A Fork in the Road

Herbert Edgar Douglass

Books by Herbert Edgar Douglass

If I Had One Sermon to Preach (anthology)

Why I Joined

What Ellen White Has Meant to Me (anthology)

We Found This Truth

Perfection: The Impossible Possibility (co-author)

Why Jesus Waits

Jesus—The Benchmark of Humanity (co-author)

Faith, Saying Yes to God

Parable of the Hurricane

The End

How to Survive the 80s (co-author)

Rediscovering Joy (Philippians and Corinthians)

Messenger of the Lord (college/seminary textbook)

How to Survive in the 21st Century

Should We Ever Say, "I Am Saved"?

God at Risk

Feast Days

They Were There (stories of EGW's visions and the people affected)

Truth Matters (an evaluation of Rick Warren's Purpose-Driven Ministry)

Never Been This Late Before

Dramatic Events Predicted by Ellen White

Love Finds a Way (a devotional)

A Fork in the Road

Questions on Doctrine: The Historic Adventist Divide of 1957

Herbert Edgar Douglass

"Though all the winds of doctrine were let loose to play upon the earth, so Truth be in the field, we do ingloriously, by licensing and prohibiting, to misdoubt her strength. Let her and Falsehood grapple: who ever knew Truth put to the worse in a free and open encounter?"—John Milton

Published by Remnant Publications, Inc.
649 E. Chicago Rd.
Coldwater, MI 49036
www.RemnantPublications.com

Editing by Ken McFarland
Cover design by Haley Trimmer
Page design by Page One Communications

"But what matter," said Charmides, "from whom I heard this?" "No matter at all," I replied: "for the point is not who said the words, but whether they are true or not."—Socrates

ISBN: 978-1-933291-18-5

Contents

Dedication

To those who weathered the heat and the fog of the last fifty years: Robert H. Pierson, Ralph Larson, Neal E. Wilson, Robert Wieland, Enoch Oliveira, C. Mervyn Maxwell, Paul Heubach, Leo Van Dolson, and Kenneth H. Wood.

What Readers Are Saying

Herb Douglass was the youngest member of the editorial team that produced the *Seventh-day Adventist Bible Commentary* (1953–1957). As such, he was an eyewitness of the drama surrounding the publication of *Questions on Doctrine* in 1957 and the controversy that followed in the 1960s. Having reflected on these events and issues for fifty years, Douglass, now an elder statesman in Adventism, shares his personal experiences and insights into the history of QOD and the ongoing quest for an adequate theology of the humanity of the Savior. No study of the QOD story is complete without Douglass's perspective.

—Jerry Moon, Ph.D., Associate Professor of Church History,
Seventh-day Adventist Theological Seminary, Andrews University

It started as a worthy project to answer a church critic who was writing a book on cults and intended to include Adventists. It ended up as a very extensive treatise on church doctrine. Unfortunately, some of the concepts published in book form were never considered mainstream Adventist theology before that time. In fact, some believe that *Questions on Doctrine* broke new ground and introduced concepts foreign to the message and mission of Seventh-day Adventists. It may even contain heretical concepts, they say. In any case, this book has divided our theological understanding as have few others. It may have in fact sowed the seeds for a diluted proclamation seen so often today in our churches. It is important that we hear from someone in the middle of the debate at the time, and no one is more qualified to share that perspective than Herb Douglass. This book is a must read for anyone who has an interest in understanding the competing concepts at work in Adventism.

—Thomas J. Mostert, President,
Pacific Union Conference of Seventh-day Adventists

My deceased father and mother, Ralph and Jeanne Larson, publicly objected to *Questions on Doctrine* because they believed that portions of it are 1) historically inaccurate and 2) theologically inept. My mentors at Loma Linda University—Paul Heubach, A. Graham Maxwell, Jack Provonsha, and Dalton Baldwin—treated it with quiet disdain for the same

reasons, even though their doctrinal reservations varied. It is now clear to everyone that they were all correct on the historical issues. The jury is still out on the theological ones, and it may never be possible to render a unanimous verdict. But I anticipate that eventually, most will conclude that they were all right about this too. In this long-needed volume, Herbert Douglass, who was there at the time, recounts what happened. We all should ponder his informative and fascinating report!

—David Larson, D.Min., Ph.D., Professor of Religion and Ethical Studies, School of Religion, Loma Linda University

In this volume Dr. Douglass has set forth solid facts dealing with Seventh-day Adventist Church history in the 1950s. He was there when the events happened. He interacted with the church leaders who were involved with the events as they happened. Because of this, his detailed account has special value. It has the authority that goes with being an "eyewitness." And I was there too, so I can attest to the accuracy of his account.

Some facts that Dr. Douglass reports are sad, for they suggest that much of the theological division of the past fifty years might have been avoided. If the church's leading theologian had been invited to participate in the dialogue with the evangelicals, if the writers of *Questions on Doctrine* had understood better how strong was the Calvinist influence on the theology of the evangelicals, if quotations from Ellen White had been presented fairly in the Appendix of QOD, . . . but why speculate? Today we live with the results, and it is important that we learn whatever lessons may be gleaned from what happened half a century ago.

One thing is certain. Facts are stubborn. Like seeds dropped into fertile soil, they may be out of sight for a while, but in time they will germinate and rise to the surface. Some generation will deal honestly and courageously with the facts set forth in this book. May God impress someone who reads this book to do just that, and thus contribute to answering Christ's prayer "that they all may be one" (John 17:21).

—Kenneth H. Wood, retired editor of the *Adventist Review* and presently chairman of the Ellen G. White Estate

Introduction

The time between 1957–2007 has been called "the most destabilizing" period in the history of the Adventist Church.[1] Why? Because of the publication of the book *Questions on Doctrine*![2]

George Knight, editor of the historical and theological introduction, Annotated Edition of *Questions on Doctrine*[3] in 2003, wrote that "*Questions on Doctrine* easily qualifies as the most divisive book in Seventh-day Adventist history. A book published to help bring peace between Adventism and conservative Protestantism, its release brought prolonged alienation and separation to the Adventist factions that grew up around it."[4]

From October 24–27, 2007, at the 50th Anniversary Conference on the Publication of *Questions on Doctrine* (QOD), at Andrews University, Berrien Springs, Michigan, twenty-four representative scholars, including a Baptist and a Presbyterian, contributed their thoughts on this notable 1957 publication. Obviously, no one person could encompass all the issues on everyone's mind. During those few days, a remarkable unanimity of respect and appreciation for each other dominated the conference.

However, most participants were not even born or were still in high school in 1957. But I was there. I knew all the principal players very well; more so as the years went by. I don't have to read someone else's opinions to understand what occurred during those crucial years.

While I was one of the assistant editors in the development of the *Seventh-day Adventist Bible Commentary* from 1955–1957, the editing process of QOD was being done in the Book Department of the Review and Herald Publishing Association, under the direction of Merwin Thurber, Book Editor. Merwin's office was only a few doors away from the *Commentary* suite.

---

1. Malcolm Bull and Keith Lockhart, *Seeking a Sanctuary—Seventh-day Adventism and the American Dream* (Bloomington, Indiana: Indiana University Press, 2007), 106.
2. *Seventh-day Adventists Answers Questions on Doctrine* (Washington, D.C: Review and Herald Publishing Association, 1957).
3. George R. Knight, Notes with Historical and Theological Introduction, *Questions on Doctrine* (Berrien Springs, MI: Andrews University Press, 2003), viii.
4. Ibid., xiii.

About every day he would bring to us the growing manuscript sent over by R. A. Anderson, L. E. Froom, and W. E. Read, co-authors of QOD. Merwin could see that the manuscript was relating to classic Adventist theology in ways that deviated from the clarity that he was used to and thus wanted input from the *Commentary* editors. Merwin's own reputation as the chief publishing house editor was on the line as it never had been before. When the co-authors had the General Conference Committee declare that no more editing needed to be done, Merwin's responsibility ceased, and QOD was *not published but printed on a job-basis only* by the Review and Herald Publishing Association.

This small volume includes my presentation at the 2007 conference, plus appendices that seem to be helpful in understanding "the explosive issues opened up by *Questions on Doctrine*."[5] Although most everyone applauded the 1957 book for about everything else, the "explosive" response focused on the rewriting of Adventist thinking on the humanity of Jesus and the limited, inadequate presentation of the Adventist sanctuary doctrine.

Although Milton L. Andreasen, Adventism's leading theologian for years, seemed to be the most alarmed by what he saw developing (even before the book's publication), a vocal chorus of leading Adventists soon developed in support of his consternation. Though retired, Andreasen had not lost his intellectual vigor. His concerns were privately leveled at the QOD trio, as well as his appeals to the president of the General Conference. When his counsel was virtually ignored, he later shared his concerns with fellow church members. Those concerns formed the crux of the "explosive" issues that brought widespread "division" within the Adventist Church for fifty years.

It is my hope that, in the following pages, a clearer understanding of the real issues that arose in 1957 can be reviewed. Further, it is also my hope, then, that the key issues mentioned above can be unambiguously grasped as essential, classic Adventism that best unfolds the larger issues that will help settle the cosmic controversy between God and Satan.

Herbert Edgar Douglass
Lincoln Hills, California
January 25, 2008

"But the wisdom that is from above is first pure, then peaceable, gentle, willing to yield, full of mercy and good fruits, without partiality and without hypocrisy. Now the fruit of righteousness is sown in peace by those who make peace" (James 3:17, 18, NKJV).

---

5. Ibid., xi.

Does Any of This Matter?

The answer is a thundering Yes!

Some have wondered if understanding why Jesus came as a babe (as all men and women come into this world) *really matters*. They say that a farmer along the Nile in Egypt, or a young man in the Sudan, or a young woman in college, have greater things on their mind than getting it straight about Christ's humanity—as long as they know that Jesus died for them.

Good thoughts! But what young and old the world over need to know more than anything else that seems so pressing is this: Is there Someone, Somewhere, who understands my predicament, my struggles, my fading hopes? If Jesus is the One, then what can I expect Him to do about what I am facing tonight and tomorrow?

The plea continues: If Jesus is still the Almighty God and the Prince of Peace, how does that theological knowledge make any difference to me? I pulled an "A" in every Bible class I ever took! And I am a great reader. Yet, what does it matter if Jesus came as Adam was before he sinned? Or, if instead, He came, inheriting the DNA of His ancestors, with all their human liabilities? In other words, so what?

However, if Jesus came without *really* experiencing the fragility and stress of ordinary human beings, it would be like holding Barry Bonds up to a struggling baseball player in high school or anywhere else—and then being told: "See Barry? It can be done! Try harder!"

Or, others will say, "If He came exactly like us with all the weaknesses of the human genetic stream, then He would have sinned as we all do—and then He also would have needed a Savior."

The truth is: Jesus did become a magnificent human being, hitting home runs every day—but He never struck out! And He did become like us "in every respect" (Hebrews 2:17, RSV), yet He remained connected to the Holy Spirit by choice—*even as we can*—and thus also become "overcomers,"

even "as I [Jesus] overcame and sat down with My Father on His throne" (Revelation 3:21).

After all, the reason Jesus came to earth was not only to die for our sins, but also to show the world of sinners how to let the Holy Spirit help them overcome their sins and walk as He walked. That is the double emphasis and heart of the New Testament. That is the joy of salvation, here and now!

It does matter as to what you think about Jesus, who prayed His way through Gethsemane and endured the Cross. Jesus experienced every human slight and rejection, from His earliest years until He returned to Heaven. He knew the pain of life, whether loneliness—or the raging fury of blood poisoning as it drained His physical forces. He was a man who appreciated the sexual drives He Himself had put into Adam and Eve, but He knew how to control them for a higher purpose. He shared every human experience, as a child through adulthood, *not vicariously but in reality!*

When one prays today, whether in kindergarten or in a university, or as a young man or woman anywhere, Jesus knows exactly what is tugging his or her mind, for "we do not have a High Priest who cannot sympathize with our weaknesses, but was in all points tempted as we are, yet without sin [because He chose not to sin].Let us therefore come boldly to the throne of grace, that we may obtain mercy [pardon] and find grace [power] to help in time of need" (Hebrews 4:15, 16).

When you need to have your gallbladder checked, you don't go to your lawyer! You go to the man or woman who knows plenty about gallbladders! When you need immediate and expert help with your moral choices, you go to Jesus, who has been here and knows what He needed to think clearly and to decide properly.

Where did He go for help? To the Holy Spirit, His constant Companion, "who in the days of His flesh, when He had offered up prayers and supplications, with vehement cries and tears to Him . . .[who] heard because of His godly fear" (Hebrews 5:7).

What did He hear? Exactly what He wants to pass on to you—the same clear-cut thoughts and divine impulse from one brain cell to another that will also make you into an overcomer. That wonderful exchange is what each of us can expect from our prayers today. You are talking to One who has been there, where you are at this very moment, and knows precisely what you need to take the next step.

That's why getting the humanity of Jesus "just right" makes all the difference in the world!

About the Book Title

Both the title of this book (*A Fork in the Road*) and the subtitle (*Questions on Doctrine: The Historic Adventist Divide of 1957*) suggest the idea of two—where once was one.

So too does the author's metaphor—which he used to great effect in his original presentation of this material at the *Questions on Doctrine* 50th Anniversary Conference at Andrews University in October of 2007—of two clashing tectonic plates. In other places, he described what happened following the publication of QOD as an earthquake.

Whatever the metaphor employed to describe the legacy of *Questions on Doctrine,* its impact on Seventh-day Adventist theology has been profound. So much so, that perhaps it's only understandable that no one metaphor can capture the extent to which this one book would affect Adventist thinking even a half century after its publication.

"God means that truth shall be brought to the front and become the subject of examination and discussion, even through the contempt placed upon it. The minds of the people must be agitated; every controversy, every reproach, every effort to restrict liberty of conscience, is God's means of awakening minds that otherwise might slumber."

—Ellen White,
The Mount of Blessing, p. 33.

♦ ONE ♦

Early Warning Signs: Two Tectonic Plates

In editing the Annotated Edition of *Questions on Doctrine,* George Knight spoke for many in his usual fresh way, when he wrote that QOD became the most divisive book in the Adventist world over the last fifty years.[1] Many believe that denominational confusion in the Seventh-day Adventist Church ever since has been the devastating price paid for this theological detour.[2] Those who think otherwise have been in an historic/ theologic coma.

My limited assignment at the *Questions on Doctrine* 50th Anniversary Conference held October 24–27 of 2007 at Andrews University in Berrien Springs, Michigan, was to answer two questions: *What happened—and why!*

The fundamental problem in 1955–1957 was that the participants unwittingly tried to merge two different theological systems without realizing all the ramifications of doing so. When Adventists try to overlay their theology on the Evangelical grid, warning lights and buzzers should be going off—many areas simply won't fit. Neither the Evangelicals nor the Adventists seemed to see some of the basic doctrines that created this Grand Canyon between Calvinism and the Adventist form of Arminianism.[3]

From another perspective, Adventists did not realize that they had certain aspects of their tectonic plate that couldn't perfectly merge with the Calvinist tectonic plate. In the attempt to close that difference, the plates

clashed, and a theological earthquake jarred both worlds—the debris of which is still settling today.[4]

In discussing the far-reaching effect of *Questions on Doctrine* with a union conference committee recently, I was not surprised, just sad. Some of the reaction was, "That was long ago, Herb. We are more interested in today and the future." Or, "That was decided by our brethren years ago—why try to go over it again?"

Among other issues, when I suggested that most independent ministries that thrive in our churches today exist because of what happened in 1957, I got more blank looks—but also a new interest to hear more! Every cause has an effect, and nothing is without cause. And that is why the 50th anniversary conference on the publication of QOD took time to look at cause and effect of probably the most "divisive" book in Adventist history.

Began With a Friendly Letter

The whole QOD dance began with a letter of special appreciation (November 28, 1949) from T. E. Unruh, president of the East Pennsylvania Conference of Seventh-day Adventists, to Dr. Donald Barnhouse, editor of the influential *Eternity* magazine, after hearing his radio address on "righteousness by faith" in 1949. Barnhouse was astonished that an Adventist leader would commend *him,* when Barnhouse was convinced that Adventists believed in "righteousness by *works.*" Barnhouse also noted that Adventists had a "satanic and dangerous" Christology.[5]

But Unruh hung in with several exchanges of letters. In one of them he enclosed *Steps to Christ,* "affirming the Evangelical character of Adventist doctrine." And Barnhouse fired back in an *Eternity* article on "How to Read Religious Books," stating that *Steps* was "false in all its parts," bearing the "mark of the counterfeit" from the first page. He also charged that *Steps to Christ* promoted "universalism. . . half-truths and Satanic error. . . so much emphasis on God's love to unregenerate men smacked of universalism."[6] Unruh decided there was no point in continuing the correspondence. No further communication took place between Unruh and Barnhouse from June 1950 until 1955.

Another thread was also being weaved into the big picture when E. Schuyler English, chairman of the Revision Committee of the Scofield Reference Bible, wrote a January 1955 editorial in his *Our Hope* magazine. He stated erroneously that Seventh-day Adventists "deny Christ's Deity" and that we "disparage the Person and work of Christ." He based the latter expression on the fact that some of our literature used the expression, "partook of our sinful, fallen nature."

Froom wrote immediately to English, contending that "the old . . . minority-view note in *Bible Readings*—contending for an inherent sinful, fallen nature for Christ—had years before been expunged because of its error, and again furnishing incontrovertible evidence to sustain these statements."[7]

English subsequently acknowledged that he had made "mistakes through the columns of *Our Hope*" regarding Adventists. When he still contended that Christ "did not partake of the fallen sinful nature of other men," Froom assured him that this "is precisely what we likewise believe." Then Froom footnoted this sentence with a typical misuse of Ellen White comments allegedly supporting his viewpoint.[8]

Now enters Walter Martin, a young researcher with a reputation in the Evangelical world as a specialist in non-Christian cults and one of Barnhouse's consulting editors on *Eternity.* He was finishing up his next book on *The Rise of the Cults,* in which he categorized Seventh-day Adventists as one of "The Big Five"—Jehovah's Witnesses, Christian Science, Mormonism, Unity, and Seventh-day Adventists.[9] But it seems that the Holy Spirit was urging him to check his facts once more regarding Adventists, because he wanted to treat them fairly. Martin turned to Toby Unruh, because he had been reading the correspondence between Unruh and Barnhouse of five years before.[10]

Martin knew of LeRoy Froom for his impressive major work on the history of prophetical interpretation.[11] He asked Unruh for a meeting in Washington, D.C., where he could interview Froom and other leaders in preparation for his upcoming book on the cults.

The rest is history. The stage was set for a frank, open discussion on the vital issues that troubled Martin and Barnhouse. Unruh and Froom asked Walter Read, a field secretary of the General Conference and biblical linguist, to join them, believing that this was a dramatic moment in Adventist history to improve the Adventist image with Evangelicals. A short time later, Roy Allan Anderson, editor of *Ministry,* was asked to join the study group.[12] These conferences began in March 1955 and ended in May 1956.

"Eternal Verities"

The Adventist trio responded to Martin's questions with a list that Froom called "the eternal verities"—"*eternal pre-existence and complete Deity of Christ,* His miraculous conception and virgin birth and sinless life during the Incarnation, His *vicarious atoning death on the Cross*—once for all and all-sufficient—His literal resurrection and ascension, His Mediation before the Father, *applying the benefits of the completed Act of Atone-*

ment He had made on the Cross and climaxing with His personal, premillennial Second Advent, which we firmly believe to be near, but without setting a time."[13]

In a further presentation he listed certain doctrines that only some of the Evangelical churches would agree with, such as: "baptism by immersion, the seventh-day Sabbath, free will, conditional immortality, and the complete annihilation of the wicked in the end-time."

Then the Adventist trio presented a third group of five doctrines that appeared to be unique to Adventism, such as: the heavenly sanctuary and Christ's two-phase ministry in it, the investigative judgment, the Spirit of prophecy as manifested in Ellen G. White's ministry, the seal of God and mark of the beast, and the three angels' messages of Revelation 13. These five were designated to be distinguishing characteristics of Seventh-day Adventists.[14]

While saying all this, Martin soon saw that what he was now hearing was "a totally different picture from what [he] had fancied and expected."[15] It seemed to deny many teachings that he had ascribed to Adventists "*because of his reading of Adventist literature*." Not many hours went by before Martin told the Adventists that "you folks are not heretics as we thought but rather redeemed brethren in Christ." He, of course, was focusing on Froom's list of "eternal verities," while recognizing that some of the second list were also believed by some Evangelical churches.[16]

Double Challenge.

For Martin, his challenge was that he had been commissioned by Zondervan Publishing to finish his book on the cults that was to include Adventists.[17] For the Adventist trio, they had the burden of explaining to the Adventist Church why certain books and doctrinal points of the past were to be purged, hoping that church members would understand that their answers to Martin were expressed in ways that Evangelicals could understand.

At that point began the attempt to merge two theological tectonic plates. Froom, Read, and Anderson convinced Martin and Barnhouse that the troublesome issues such as the human nature of Christ and the larger view of the atonement were, as Barnhouse wrote, the products of "the lunatic fringe as there are similar wild-eyed irresponsibles in every field of fundamental Christianity."[18]

The fat was in the fire! At least M. L. Andreasen, long-time Adventism's leading theologian, read Barnhouse's article and found himself among the

"lunatic fringe," along with most other Adventist writers who emphasized the human experience of Jesus and His two-phased atonement.

The "Lunatic Fringe"

Obviously, after Barnhouse had made this charge, whatever else the Adventist trio would write would be suspect and would have to be "met" with Adventist vigor. This accusation of a "lunatic fringe" was incredible when we take a quick look at those who did believe that Jesus took on Himself sinful flesh to live a sinless life. Think about the following list of prominent "lunatic" Adventist leaders: Francis Nichol, W. H. Branson, Ray Cottrell, Don Neufeld (all living in Washington, D.C. during the 1950s) as well as a century of Adventist leadership, such as E. J. Waggoner, A. T. Jones, S. N. Haskell, W. W. Prescott, Uriah Smith, M. C. Wilcox, G. W. Reaser, G. B. Thompson, M. E. Kern, C. M. Snow, C. P. Bollman, Meade MacGuire, C. B. Haynes, I. H. Evans, L. A. Wilcox. William Wirth, E. F. Hackman, A. G. Daniells, Oscar Tait, Allen Walker, Merlin Neff, W. E. Howell, Gwynne Dalrymple, T. M French, J. L. McElhany, C. Lester Bond, E. K. Slade, J. E. Fulton, D. H. Kress, Frederick Lee, L. H. Wood, A. V. Olson, Christian Edwardson, J. C. Stevens, F. M. Wilcox, A. W. Truman, F. G. Clifford, Varner Johns, Dallas Young, J. B. Conley, Fenton Edwin Froom, W. E. Read, J. A. McMillan, Benjamin Hoffman, H. L. Rudy, including the writings of M. L. Andreasen and the hundreds of times that Ellen White unambiguously wrote that Jesus "accepted the results of the great law of heredity . . . to share our sorrows and temptations, and to give us the example of a sinless life."[19]

If Only. . .

If only both sides had stepped back for a quiet moment, they would have realized that they were both shooting at moving targets. They stood on two separate tectonic plates attempting to merge, setting up earthquakes that would reverberate for at least fifty years. If Froom had not had a short fuse and a driving premise that obscured his normal historical nose for truth, and if Anderson had not been so excited about what seemed to be a monumental public relations scoop—we would not have had the QOD earthquake.

Strange as it now appears, if Froom had not early on so quickly dismissed the results of his own informal poll among Adventist leaders regarding their understanding of Christ's human nature, he may have avoided the developing earthquake. In the answers to his poll he discovered that "nearly all of them had that idea" [that Christ had a "sinful nature]"[20] In Froom's letter to R. R. Figuhr, president of the General Conference, he blamed this unfortunate situation on these leaders being "too weak in the-

ology and in giving the right impression to others."[21] Friend Froom was simply wearing blinders caused by personal assumptions, while Figuhr was intimidated by Froom's august stature as the long-time editor of *Ministry* magazine.[22]

Notes:

1. Annotated Edition, *Questions on Doctrine* (Berrien Springs, MI: Andrews University Press), 2003, xiii.
2. Malcolm Bull and Keith Lockhart, *Seeking a Sanctuary,* Second Edition (Bloomington, IN: Indiana University Press, 2007), 106: "*Questions on Doctrine* raised uncertainties about what Adventists actually believed that made the Evangelical era that followed the most destabilizing in the church's history."
3. Adventists part with Wesleyan Arminianism in (1) their understanding of the immortal soul notion that has much to do with one's understanding of the atonement and the doctrine of sin, and (2) how to fully understand John 3:16: was it a gift to be accepted, or an offer to be sought—or both?
4. I am indebted to many through the years who have wrestled with the impact of QOD on Adventist thinking. I am particularly grateful for Julius Nam's remarkable doctoral dissertation, "Reactions to the Seventh-day Adventist Evangelical Conferences and *Questions on Doctrine* 1955–1971." Others who have been extremely thorough in their analyses through the years include Kenneth Wood, Jerry Moon, Ralph Larson, Ken McFarland, Robert Hancock, Sr., Leroy Moore, Jean Zurcher, Kevin Paulson, William Grotheer, Larry Kirkpatrick, Woody Whidden, and George Knight.
5. Donald Grey Barnhouse, "Are Seventh-day Adventists Christians? A New Look at Seventh-day Adventism," *Eternity,* September 1956; T. E. Unruh, The Seventh-day Adventist Evangelical Conferences of 1955–1956, *Adventist Heritage,* fourth quarter, 1977.
6. Barnhouse, "Spiritual Discernment, or How to Read Religious Books, *Eternity,* June 1950.
7. *Movement of Destiny* (Washington, D.C.: Review and Herald Publishing Association, 1971), 469.
8. *Ibid.* 470.
9. Walter R. Martin *The Rise of the Cults* (Grand Rapids, MI: Zondervan, 1955), 12.
10. Unruh, Adventist *Heritage, op cit.*
11. L. E. Froom, *The Prophetic Faith of Our Fathers* (Washington, D.C: Review and Herald, 1950). Four volumes.
12. Unruh, *op. cit.*
13. Froom, *Movement of Destiny* (Washington, D.C., Review and Herald Publishing Association, 1971), 478. Emphasis in original.
14. Julius Nam, "Reactions to the Seventh-day Adventist Evangelical Conferences and *Questions on Doctrine* 1955–1971, 57. Doctoral dissertation, Andrews University, 2005, 54, 55.
15. Froom, *Movement of Destiny,* 479.

16. Julius Nam, "Reactions to the Seventh-day Adventist Evangelical Conferences and *Questions on Doctrine* 1955–1971, 57. Doctoral dissertation, Andrews University, 2005.

17. Froom, *op. cit.,* 480.

18. Barnhouse, *Eternity,* September 1957.

19. Ellen G. White, *The Desire of Ages,* 49. "Clad in the vestments of humanity, the Son of God came down to the level of those He wished to save. In Him was no guile or sinfulness; He was ever pure and undefiled; yet He took upon Him our sinful nature." *Review and Herald,* Dec. 15, 1896. "He took upon His sinless nature our sinful nature that He might know how to succor those that are tempted."—Ellen G. White, *Medical Ministry,* 181.

20. Nam, op. cit., 66.

21. Ibid., 67.

22. L. E. Froom (1890–1974), secretary of General Conference Ministerial Association from 1926–1950. During this time, he founded *Ministry* magazine and was its editor for twenty-two years.

♦ TWO ♦

Basic Flaw on the Part of Both Parties

Calvinism and Arminianism—two tectonic plates—were about to collide. Even as Earth scientists have warning systems in the ground that can help predict the collision of moving plates, so keen theologians should have warning systems in place. When Adventists try to impose their theological structure onto Evangelical Calvinism, warning lights in computers should be going off, before huge, unintended consequences develop for both parties—and vice versa. Many contemporary Evangelicals tried to warn Barnhouse and Martin of what was happening, but only time would have to tell the full story[1]

Evangelical Calvinism is the theological tree of most Evangelicals, although some Evangelicals try to graft some branches onto the Arminian tree.[2] The Calvinism tree has its roots in a partial picture of God—God only as Sovereign—but sovereign in such a way that all that happens in this world is fore-ordained or predestinated. Thus, only some men and women are elected to be saved; others are not; they go to an eternally burning hell. The idea of human responsibility is eliminated—God wills the future for everyone, because no one can possibly thwart God's will.

Calvinism Rooted in Augustine

Calvinism's roots are nurtured by Augustine's theology, who is considered by many as antiquity's greatest theologian and to whom Roman Catholicism

is also greatly indebted.[3] Augustine's logical but ill-conceived presuppositions began with his huge major premise of the Sovereignty of God[4] that led to his innovative notions concerning original sin and man's total depravity. In turn, these particular notions infused those who followed him from the sixth century A. D., through Aquinas and into the Reformation, to our day.[5]

"Five Points"

Calvinists reduce their theology to the famous Five Points, all emanating from the core doctrine of their understanding of the sovereignty of God.

1. Total depravity of mankind (all men and women are born sinners).
2. Unconditional election (some are elected to be saved; others are not).
3. Limited atonement (Christ died for only the elect).
4. Irresistible grace (men and women who are elected are given the "gift" of faith).
5. Perseverance of the saints ("once saved, always saved").

Arminians begin with their roots in the soil of freedom, out of which develops all aspects of the Great Controversy between God and Satan. Because God made men and women out of love, for love, and to live in love, Arminians clash with Calvinists on every main issue concerning responsibility in salvation. However, most Arminians, lacking the integrity of a coherent theology, have many viewpoints in common with Calvinists, such as total depravity, Sunday being the Sabbath of the fourth commandment, and the soul being immortal, leading to an ever-burning hell and other biblical inconsistencies.

But the concept of human responsibility (synergism) in response to the love of God became the fundamental, core truth for Arminians in their sixteenth-century response to Roman Catholics and Calvinism. And Calvinists repaid their response with incredible cruelty! Predestination (implicit monergism) was, for the Arminians, unbiblical. They accepted the biblical message that Jesus indeed died for sinners, all sinners, not just for the selected few. For them, the decision to be a follower of Christ was the response of a thoughtful man or woman, thus leading to the rejection of infant baptism, among other differences.

Further, for Arminians, those finally lost or unsaved are those who reject 1) God's offer to forgive them and 2) God's power to live a transformed

life. Thus, for most Arminians sanctification is as important as justification—a point rejected by Calvinists because it didn't fit their rigid straitjacket of predestination—human performance for them didn't matter. Even further, Arminians are not forced into Calvinism's straitjacket that assumed Christ's work on Calvary alone to be sufficient for salvation and that His work as High Priest had nothing to do with preparing men and women eventually to be saved.

Forensic-only Salvation

Calvinism's straitjacket led to "forensic-only salvation," which has troubled the Christian church for 400 years. *Forensic justification* is another term for *penal substitution,* wherein, in some way, (1) God's wrath is appeased in the death of Jesus, and 2) the sinner is forgiven by "faith" that is denuded from any relationship to character change in the process. This unbiblical notion has confused the works of grace and the meaning of "righteousness by faith."[6] This confusion has been at the bottom of divisions in the Adventist Church since the 1960s. For many, it became monomania.

Adventist Trio's Fatal Flaw

One of the major issues that seemed to elude Froom, Anderson, and Read was that Adventists do not fit into either the Calvinist tectonic plate or Arminian tectonic plate. Here was their fatal flaw—they were unprepared to portray the gestalt of classic Adventism!

For instance, Adventists differ with Calvinists and many Arminians in regard to the nature of mankind; that is, we do not believe that we possess an immortal soul, which immediately involves one's concept of original sin and/or the kind of body/mind with which human beings are born.

Again, because we have a more complete understanding of why Jesus is our High Priest, Adventists think carefully about how His High Priestly work directly affects one's salvation and one's preparation to be entrusted with eternal life. That is, the QOD trio did not make exceedingly clear to Martin and Barnhouse how our Lord's Cross and High Priestly ministries are two equal parts of His atonement that directly affect our human responsibility in the redemption process. More about this later.

Further, because Adventists, almost unanimously, for a century prior to 1955, accepted the biblical counsel that Jesus was born a human being, "in every respect," and "that He was in all points tempted as we are, yet without sin" (Hebrews 2:17; 4:15), they had believed that Jesus met and defeated Satan's fiery darts in the same way He asks us to—by trusting in the Holy Spirit's intervention in our lives. He showed us how to live and die so

that we can eventually be entrusted with eternal life. This too was under-emphasized with Martin and Barnhouse—an unfortunate failure on the part of the Adventist trio.

Principle Issues

In other words: the principal issues in the 1955–1957 tectonic earthquake were clear-cut: 1) differences regarding sin, original sin and its implications and 2) conditionalism and free will—all of which affected (a) one's understanding of Christ's humanity, (b) the multiple aspects of His atonement, and c) the consequences of all this on one's eschatology. Above all, one's understanding of sin and the nature of man is the "issue underneath all other issues"—the key to Adventist theological taxonomy.

Adventist Trio Were Highly Respected Leaders

How could all this happen? We say this with complete respect for our Adventist friends:

R. A. Anderson was a revered homiletician and public evangelist. His preaching became a mountaintop experience for large audiences on several continents. During the 1950s he was editor of *Ministry,* the monthly magazine that all Adventist leaders and pastors would avidly read. But he was not a trained theologian.

W. E. Read knew his biblical languages and was a highly respected and valued church administrator— but not trained in systematic theology. Framed by his white goatee, we enjoyed his slight whistle when he softly spoke. And he and Froom labored with less than mutual trust.[7]

Leroy Froom was well known in Christian circles as an indefatigable researcher. His major contributions, *The Prophetic Faith of Our Fathers* and *The Conditionalist Faith of Our Fathers*[8], became benchmarks for scholars in many denominations. His productive capacity was enormous; his towering energy made him a leader in any conversation. But, he too was over his head in systematic theology.

Personal Friends

These were remarkable men, highly respected. Anderson and Froom became my strong, life-long friends. In the 1970s, while I was associate editor of the *Review and Herald,* Froom would visit me periodically to discuss current events in the world and in the church. He knew exactly where I stood theologically because of my weekly editorials that deliberately focused on the flaws in QOD—but theological positions did not interfere with our friendship. Froom aged gracefully. When he was dying at the age

of 84, in the Sligo Nursing Home (Takoma Park, MD) I was probably one of the last persons to stroke his hand. I treasure his memory.

Anderson and I had a father/son relationship. He ate in our home; our children were impressed. In his retirement, especially after his move to Loma Linda, he would call periodically—at least every month. With his famous voice now weak and raspy, he would invariably ask, "Herb, what is happening to our church?" I never did have the courage to suggest that most of the problems he was troubled with started with the publishing of QOD. Elder Anderson died in 1985 at the age of 90—a model preacher and wholesome friend.

But the facts are that our Adventist trio, untrained as theologians, was no match for Martin and Barnhouse, specialists in Calvinistic Evangelicalism. What made the situation in 1955 even thornier was the deliberate decision to ignore M. L. Andreasen, the senior Adventist theologian for decades.[9] Andreasen had been head of the Systematic Theology department of the Adventist seminary for years, retiring in 1949. He had written numerous articles and at least thirteen books, some of which have never been surpassed.[10] Well-known as an authority on the sanctuary doctrine, he was the author of the section on the book of Hebrews in the *Seventh-day Adventist Commentary.*

I can heartily affirm Dr. Knight's penetrating statement in his "Introduction to the Annotated Edition" of QOD: "Looking back, one can only speculate on the different course of Adventist history *if* Andreasen had been consulted regarding the wording of the Adventist position on the atonement, *if* Froom and his colleagues hadn't been divisive in the handling of issues related to the human nature of Christ, *if* both Froom and Andreasen would have had softer personalities."[11] Probably, it could not have been said any better!

Notes:

1. I was and still am grateful for the courage and gracious spirit of both Barnhouse and Martin. As soon as Martin's book, *The Truth About Seventh-day Adventism* (Grand Rapids: Zondervan, 1960) was published (with Barnhouse's Foreword), scathing reviews appeared in books and magazine articles. These well-known but unconvinced writers included John W. Sanderson, *Westminster Theological Journal* 23, (1960); Merrill Tenney, *Eternity,* May 1960; Frank A. Lawrence, *Christianity Today,* July 4, 1960; John Gerstner, *The Theology of the Major Sects*; Herbert S. Bird, *Theology of Seventh-Day Adventism,*1961; Norman F. Douty, *Another Look at Seventh-day Adventism,* 1962; Russell P. Spittler, *Cults and Isms: Twenty Alternates to Evangelical Christianity,* 1962; J. Oswald Sanders, *Heresies and Cults,* revised, 1962; Jan Karel Van Baalen, *The Chaos of Cults,* 4th rev. and expanded,1962;Anthony A. Hoekema, *The Four Major Cults,*1963; Gordon R. Lewis, *Confronting the Cults,*1966; and Irving Robertson, *What*

the Cults Believe, 1966. I found it more than interesting that none of these books were published by Zondervan Publishing, the publisher of Martin's *The Truth About Seventh-day Adventism.* In 1965, Martin published his response to the major, near-unanimous evangelical opposition to Martin and Barnhouse, in his next book, *The Kingdom of the Cults: An Analysis of the Major Cult Systems in the Present Christian Era,* 1965. He did not list Seventh-day Adventism among the twelve major non-Christian cults, but he did provide an Appendix with a lengthy overview of evangelical responses to *The Truth About Seventh-day Adventism.* For an extended review of these unsatisfied Evangelicals, see Julius Nam, *op. cit.,* 105-174.

2. For example, splitting the Evangelicals today is the "Lordship/no-Lordship salvation" controversy. Though both sides are admittedly predestinarians, the debate is virtually identical to what has tended to divide the Adventist Church for the past fifty years. Reading what John F. MacArthur, Jr. (the leading representative of Lordship salvation) teaches and then reading Zane Hodges and Charles Ryrie (leading spokesmen for no-Lordship salvation), one hears echoes of the same issues that Paul faced in the first century—and every other church leader from Paul's day to ours. (See John F. MacArthur, Jr., *Faith Works, the Gospel According to the Apostles* [Dallas: Word Publishing, 1993], especially chapter two: "A Primer on the 'Lordship Salvation' Controversy"). However, MacArthur and I differ fundamentally on the "definition of faith," which colors his defense, even though he is vastly more correct than his opponents.

3. For perhaps the latest and most inclusive biography of Augustine, see James J. O'Donnell, *Augustine* (HarperCollins Publishers, 2005), 1-396.

4. Roger Olson summarized: "Augustine's God, though Trinitarian, is made captive to the Greek philosophical theology of divine simplicity, immutability, and impassibility and turns out to be more like a great cosmic emperor than a loving, compassionate heavenly Father. . . . [Theologians] ought to consider the extent to which classical Christian doctrines of God have been unduly influenced by Greek philosophical categories of metaphysical perfection." *The Story of Christian Theology: Twenty Centuries of Tradition and Reform* (Downers Grove, IL: Inter-Varsity Press, 1999), 530.

5. Probably the greatest phenomenon in Christian church history has been the magisterial role that Augustine has played in his development of the original sin notion. None of the Latin fathers before him taught that moral sin was somehow transmitted to offspring; the Eastern Church never bought into Augustine's notions. Irenaeus (c.144–c. 202), the church's first systematic theologian, clearly avoided Augustine's later conclusions. Julian and Pelagius, Augustine's contemporaries, countered his biblical exegesis regarding his use of Romans 5 especially, as all previous church fathers had interpreted that chapter and other texts Augustine had used. Pelagius, of course, was equally wrong in opining that each person is born with a clean sheet and not born with inherited weaknesses and liabilities—each person able to make moral decisions without prevenient (God-initiated) grace. Because of Augustine's immense political, oratorical, and philosophical skills, he became the recognized chief architect of orthodoxy in the Western Church. Augustine's system of theology is reflected in Calvinism, which Evangelical Protestantism generally holds in common.

6. Forensic-salvation (overemphasis on its own definition of justification) ignores 2 Thessalonians 2:13 and Titus 3:5, etc. The Bible never considers sanctification as inferior to justification—they are considered as two foci in the ellipse of truth. Ellen White said it best in a few words: "So we have nothing in ourselves of which to boast. We have no ground for self-exaltation. Our only ground of hope is in the righteousness of Christ imputed to us, and in that wrought by His Spirit working in and through us."—*Steps to Christ,* 63. "The proud heart strives to earn salvation, but both our title to heaven and

our fitness for it are found in the righteousness of Christ."—*The Desire of Ages,* 300. The basis for the "forensic-only salvation" notion rests squarely on one's understanding of original sin that, for many, pollutes all humans from birth and thus makes perfect obedience impossible. Marvin R. Vincent's *Word Studies in the New Testament,* volume III (Peabody, MA: Hendrickson Publishers, ,n.d.): "[Justification] is not, however, to be construed as indicating a mere legal transaction, or adjustment between God and man, . . .The element of character must not only not be eliminated from it; it must be foremost in it. Justification is more than pardon. Pardon is an act which frees the offender from the penalty of the law, adjusts his outward relation to the law, but does not necessarily effect any change in him personally. It is *necessary* to justification but not *identical* with it. Justification aims directly at *character.* It contemplates making *the man himself* right; that the new and right relation to God in which faith places him shall have its natural and legitimate issue in *personal rightness.* The phrase *faith is counted for righteousness,* does not mean that faith is a *substitute* for righteousness, but that faith *is* righteousness; righteousness *in the germ* indeed, but still *bona fide* righteousness. The act of faith inaugurates a righteous life and a righteous character. The man is not made inherently holy in himself, because his righteousness is derived from God; neither is he merely *declared* righteous by a legal fiction without reference to his personal character." 39, 40 (emphasis in original).

7. Nam, *op. cit.,* 70–72.
8. Froom, *The Conditionalist Faith of Our Fathers,* Vols I, II (Washington, D.C.: Review and Herald, 1965).
9. Nam., 267: "Despite his contributions as a leading theologian of the church,. . . he had not been one of some 250 who were invited to review the manuscript in September 1956."
10. Some of Andreasen's books include *The Sanctuary, The Epistle to the Hebrews, A Faith to Life By, The Faith of Jesus, What Can a Man Believe,* and *Saints and Sinners.*
11. Annotated QOD, xxvi.

♦ THREE ♦

Analysis of a Theological Impasse

Despite the "What ifs," we now work with what happened. We now realize, after 50 years, that the nuclear fallout of the 1957 QOD needs to be thoughtfully and fairly addressed. Why was the 2007 seminar on QOD more than mere history lectures? Because:

1. We owe it to a generation of pastors and administrators who have been schooled since 1957. They have been taught that the conclusions of QOD fairly represented the core beliefs of the Adventist movement.
2. And we owe it to a generation of millions of lay members who have very little clue as to the colossal issues at stake for clear Adventist thinking today. On several continents they wonder why certain theological issues still divide our church and why there are so many "independent" groups the world over.

We must heartily note before we analyze some of the imbedded theological flaws in QOD that much of QOD has served us well, such as its treatment of law and legalism, Sabbath and Sunday, Daniel 7-9, etc. Andreasen himself said that "there are so many good things in the book that may be of real help to many"[1]

But several problem areas stare us in the face! We have already noted the flaw in the mystifying reference to scores of Adventist thought leaders

who were listed as the "lunatic fringe." The second puzzling problem was the amazing maltreatment of Ellen White quotations and the unwarranted subheads used to group them. Dr. Knight analyzed this well when he noted that the 1957 QOD "creates a false impression on the human nature of Christ" and that one of the headings, that Christ *'Took Sinless Human Nature,'* especially was "problematic in that it implies that that was Ellen White's idea when in fact she was quite emphatic in repeatedly stating the Christ took 'our sinful nature,' etc.[2]

In the early 1970s while serving as one of the *Review and Herald* editors, I had the library resources to check all the QOD statements in its Appendices and Indexes. I was repeatedly shocked at the obvious bias of those who had collected the Ellen White statements. Day after day, when time permitted, I would bring the original source into Ken Wood's office (Editor-in-chief) and we would exchange our amazement and bafflement that the denomination for decades had been misled in such crucial areas. Many statements were deliberately altered with unethical use of the ellipsis (...); many were obviously used only in part, removing the clarity of the context.[3]

The third problem was the method the Adventist trio employed in using non-Adventist references to support certain positions. Fair enough. In several places, Froom used his encyclopedic knowledge of "champions of conditional immortality" to validate the Adventist position on the nature of man and our position on the immutability of the moral law.[4] But when the trio tried to defend our century-old understanding of the unique importance of Christ's human nature, they went into a fog. An immense line of Protestant scholars could have been presented to underscore this long-standing position of Adventist leaders, but not one was referred to.

Because of these valiant attempts to reconcile Calvinistic disagreements with an agreeable presentation from the Adventists, major theological issues were misconstrued. No amount of historical analysis will gloss over this theological malfeasance. *Adventists missed the opportunity of the century*! Never had Adventists been given such a platform to cheerfully clarify any misunderstanding with Protestants and to illuminate distinctive doctrines that Adventists think important—but they missed it by a couple of light years.

Obviously it could be argued that if we had laid out the logical, symbiotic interaction of Adventist beliefs, Martin and Barnhouse would have responded differently, perhaps. Perhaps QOD would not have been published!

More What Ifs!

But the "what ifs" continue. (1) *if* QOD had been winsomely clear regarding its beliefs, the Adventist church would not have spawned the plethora of troubled responses within Adventism that segued into many so-called "independent" groups. Think about these "independent ministries," dozens of them, almost all concerned with the undertreatment of two specific Adventist truths: the importance of the dual ministry of Jesus and the full humanity of Jesus as He accepted the genetic stream of His many ancestors, as any baby must.[5]

(2) Another "what if" is the theological swerve in certain Seminary instruction beginning in the 1960s. Some of the new uncertainties floating as theological germs in QOD directly led to unintended consequences in the Adventist bloodstream; a so-called "new theology" suddenly highlighted so-called "Reformation theology," muting the century-old emphasis on character transformation expected in God's loyalists. Interweaving within these new theological contours since 1957 has been an attempt to "revise" what happened in the 1888 General Conference and an attempt to reevaluate Ellen G. White—resulting in her inspirational assets being highlighted at the expense of her theological insights and contributions.

(3) Another "what if" is the phenomenal silence in the Adventist media, pulpit and classroom for the past forty years regarding a proper emphasis on traditional Adventist topics such as "the investigative judgment," "latter rain," "loud cry," "sealing work," "character determining destiny," "delay in the Advent," "why Christ's humanity is so important to a transformed life," etc.[6]

(4) What about the "what if" that never happened, such as the misleading assertions in Figuhr's article in *Ministry,* January 1958: "Probably no other book published by this denomination has been so carefully read by so large a group of responsible men of the denomination before its publication as the one under consideration. Some 250 men in American and in other countries received copies of the manuscript before it was published. The preliminary manuscript work by a group of some fourteen individuals had been so carefully prepared that only a minimum of suggestions of improvement were made. There was, however, a remarkable chorus of approval."

But, in fact, only a small number actually replied and "those who did respond supplied a number of penetrating and (even what turned out to be brilliantly prophetic) critiques."[7] (At that time, Adventists, leaders and lay members alike, were accustomed to believing the statements of contemporary leaders, especially if they were in print!) These leadership beguiling assertions were all it took to hijack a whole generation of Adventists!

Perpetuating the Myth

For instance, look at Anderson's editorial in the June, 1957 issue of *Ministry* where he perpetuated the myth: "Of all the books we have ever published, none has had more careful scrutiny than this one. . . . No manuscript has been more carefully prepared and no book has been awaited with more eager anticipation."

R. R. Figuhr, president of the General Conference writing further in the January 1958, issue of *Ministry,* made matters even more surreal, Referring to the Ellen White quotations in the appendix, he stated: "This book representing, as it does, the careful work of a large group of responsible leaders, and containing such valuable quotations from the Spirit of prophecy, is unique and, we believe, fills a needed place among our published works."

Group Think

This is a marvelous example of "group think" that anesthetized everyone in the General Conference group, 1957-1958, and for decades thereafter. In the March 1958 issue of *Ministry,* Anderson continued this nightmarish drama after repeating the enthusiastic reception that QOD received after publication.

He pointed out that while 250 denomination leaders had approved the manuscript, "except for minor suggestions, no change whatsoever in content was called for. . . . Some valuable suggestions were offered, but in no area of doctrine was any major change called for." Further, "A careful reading of *Questions on Doctrine* makes one aware that alongside the Bible is the constant confirmation of our denominational beliefs by the Spirit of prophecy. In the light of this we are surprised that a section of this book, as well as certain statements in *Ministry* has evidently been misunderstood by a very few. This is particularly surprising to us in the light of the universal appraisal that has come."

But there was more. Apparently even Anderson felt uneasy; He needed to convince himself as well as the rest of the Adventist Church, even further. He continued: "As already stated, from all parts of the world field have come expressions of heartfelt gratitude for the convincing and scholarly answers this book contains. . . . The field reveals the unanimity of our denominational beliefs, and a careful reading of *Questions on Doctrine* will reveal that it is in complete accord with the clear statements of the Spirit of prophecy, which we have had in our libraries for more than half a century."

Loma Linda Professionals

In other words, if anyone disagreed with QOD, he surely was not in the mainstream of genuine Adventism! Or did not believe in the Spirit of prophecy! This message was not lost on many around the United States. A group of prominent leaders in Loma Linda, CA, signed a very unambiguous statement charging that QOD "misrepresented "certain vital fundamentals and compromised other tenets of our faith" and that "certain statements and teachings of the book will never be accepted by a considerable number of our people. In fact, it is our conviction that not since the time of J. H. Kellogg's pantheistic controversy of more than a half century ago has anything arisen to cause such disquietude, dissension and disunity among our people as the publication of this book."[8]

Looking back, we must give the QOD trio a huge A+ for their fantastic public-relations, propaganda campaign, even before QOD was published.[9] For example, the trio did an incredible sales job in softening up Adventists on the *new slant* that chiefly focused on whether Jesus assumed "sinful nature" when He became a baby boy and whether the best way to explain the work of Jesus in the Heavenly Sanctuary was only in terms of "applying the benefits" of the Cross. (More about this later.)

In January 23, 1958, Figuhr, president of the General Conference, wrote in the *Review and Herald* that *Questions on Doctrine* had been "prepared by the General Conference by a group of our ablest scholars and approved by our leaders through the world—to clarify to the world the true evangelical nature of Adventist beliefs and teachings."[10]

On July 25, 1956, in writing to Adventist leaders worldwide, Froom said: "No more eminent or representative group could have been consulted. No more competent group could approve. And that they did."[11]

Pure fantasy!

The Mythical Mantra

I was there. I read and heard the mantra that this large group of Adventist leaders had indeed affirmed the QOD approach. Only later did the truth come out that only a very few actually responded. Nothing arrived from outside of North America; no local or union conference administrator from North America responded[12]—partly because they were stunned or, on reflection, they thought that QOD was not going anywhere.

The editors at the Review and Herald Publishing Association sent individual letters to Figuhr and to the QOD trio. Each expressed great concern for the general procedure, hoping for more biblical backup for each

of our doctrines.[13]

Cottrell's Sixteen-page Warning

The inimitable Raymond Cottrell, associate editor of the *Commentary,* would find it impossible to write only a one-page letter, especially when asked by the Review's editorial committee to respond to QOD. In his sixteen-page evaluation (November 1956) written exclusively for General Conference leaders, Cottrell listed five areas of concern: 1) the change in Adventist theology; 2) Ellen G. White; 3) the remnant church; 4) Adventism in relation to other evangelical churches; and 5) the proposed book on Adventism by Martin.[14]

(1) Cottrell declared that the evangelicals' assertion that Adventist theology had recently changed to be "a fundamental fallacy." (2) Cottrell argued that Ellen White never claimed infallibility and that "there is no intrinsic difference between the Bible and the writings of Ellen G. White as to degree of inspiration, infallibility, authoritative quality, or binding force upon the consciences and lives of Seventh-day Adventists." (3) Cottrell contended Adventists had not suddenly changed their definition of the "remnant church," still believing that they still considered their movement to be the remnant church but always appealing to others to join them. (4) Cottrell declared that no evangelical church could agree not to proselytize for no church anywhere could prevent members from switching churches. (5) Cottrell questioned the objectivity in Martin's book on Adventism, whether readers would "know where facts end and where Martin's interpretation of the facts began."

Cottrell ended his neatly developed fears regarding QOD that was still in the editing process by appealing for clarity and honesty on the part of the Adventist trio. He was fearful that Martin would feel "double-crossed" which would "lead. . . to the most intense bitterness" when he discovered that QOD did not clearly represent the Adventist mind and that he and Barnhouse had been deliberately misled.

In his closing sentences, Cottrell predicted: "Almost certainly, there will also arise a storm of opposition when our ministry and laity discover the real meaning of the actual terms on which we have achieved rapprochement with Martin and other evangelicals." He said that we should expect "a serious division" among Adventist workers when both QOD and Martin's book were published but that there was still time to "take adequate measures *now* to clear the atmosphere *before* Martin's book is published, and to set forth in [*Questions on Doctrine*] a clear exposition of [Adventism's] true position (Cottrell's emphasis)."[15]

Cottrell's warnings and suggestions did not seem to have any marked effect on the finished QOD.[16]

Nichol's Warning

Francis D. Nichol, editor of the *Review and Herald,* wrote in a confidential letter to Figuhr, that some statements were made to Martin that "many of us, on mature consideration, are unable to support." He feared that the QOD trio had "either not sensed as they should the full import of most distinctive doctrinal differences with the world, or else unwittingly succumbed to the temptation to blur deficiencies in order to find a middle ground of fellowship."[17]

However, even though some minor editing was done, QOD did not reveal any indication that the criticisms made any significant impact on the book's content. The Adventist trio won out, almost as if keen readers of the manuscript did not count. Note the extravagant language in QOD's introduction: "These answers represent the position of our denomination. . . . This volume can be viewed as truly representative."[18]

I remember as if it were yesterday when the QOD trio finally told the Review and Herald editing committee on January 30, 1957 that no more editing would be permitted. Thus, the Review and Herald Publishing Association accepted the manuscript on a "text basis," that is, the publishing house would not be providing any editorial oversight, but simply would serve as a printer and distributor. Thus they would not be held responsible for its content.[19]

Washing of Hands

That morning in the *Commentary* office, Raymond Cottrell left the room and returned with a towel over his left arm and a basin of water in his right. Then each of us on the *Commentary* staff took turns washing our hands of any more input or responsibility for QOD. We didn't know then the full implications of what we were doing together around that basin!.

Unknown to the *Commentary* Editors As Well Others

For many months prior to the printing of QOD, the covert battle was on between M. L. Andreasen and the QOD trio. Andreasen first sent his concerns privately to Figuhr who did his best to be loyal to the trio. Several editorials in *Ministry,* however, rang Andreasen's bell, setting off well-reasoned concerns. Other church leaders pled with General Conference administrators to at least let Andreasen see the manuscript before publica-

tion—all were denied. All this correspondence has been resurrected in Dr. Nam's doctoral thesis, which I hope gets published in book form soon.

Thoughful men such as Merlin Neff and Richard Lewis,[20] both book editors at the Pacific Press Publishing Association, wrote cogent concerns in defense of Andreasen. M. E. Kern, General Conference administrator,[21] speaking for others, was deeply concerned. North American leaders, such as R. R. Bietz, predicted a great disaster ahead, that "a tornado was yet to come."[22]

Theodore Carcich, president of the Central Union Conference, sent a letter to all his local conference presidents: "Under a guise of sweet-honeyed words oozing with so-called Christian fellowship, Mr. Martin proceeds to serve up the same theological hash . . . that our spiritual forefathers had to refute years ago." In his letter to Figuhr, he called QOD "a clever and subtle attempt to undermine the foundational doctrines of Seventh-day Adventists."[23]

Edward Heppenstall wrote ominously, "It will be very unfortunate, if after . . . publication, any position taken will be repudiated by a large section of the workers themselves," leading to "widespread division" and "confusion with and without."[24]

And Cottrell was even more prophetic: "Let us be certain that nothing gets into the proposed book that will take us the next 50 years to live down."[25]

Why *Commentary* Editors Did Not Speak With Louder Voices

I know some may be asking: What *if* the editors of *the SDA Bible Commentary* had reacted sooner or with a louder voice? As we have seen, the various editors did make their concerns known but not in public or in their periodicals. Why? For two specific reasons:

1) We truly never thought QOD would go anywhere. Who would buy it? But we never dreamed of the push-polling that the editors of *Ministry* would do, with the hovering blessing of the General Conference president. Many local conferences were invited, after a considerable price break, to send QOD to all their workers.

2) A larger picture served as a backdrop—editors did not want to take sides publicly because financially the Review and Herald Publishing Association had gone deep into the preparation of the *Seventh-day Adventist Bible Commentary;* we didn't want anything to limit its potential sale. In other words, we didn't think taking sides publicly on QOD was worth

jeopardizing the success and appeal of the much bigger contribution that the *Commentary* would make on the very issues that were already dividing the church. The *Bible Commentary* avoided the errors of QOD by emphasizing the classic Adventist understanding of the humanity of Christ and the purpose of the sanctified life in preparing people to live forever.

Missed the Opportunity of a Century

All these "what ifs" contributed to the nuclear fallout or, as some say, the neutron bomb of the 1957 QOD. The Adventist church had seemingly lost for a time its uniqueness as the bearer of God's last-day message to a mixed-up, terror-ridden world. In our attempts to prove our "Christianity" we muted our distinctive contribution to rediscovering the genuine roots of Christianity.

Notes:

1. Ibid.
2. Ibid., xvi.
3. I am reminded of those times when Ellen White was disappointed with those who misused her writings: "I know that many men take the testimonies the Lord has given, and apply them as they suppose they should be applied, picking out a sentence here and there, taking it from its proper connection, and applying it according to their idea." —*Selected Messages,* bk.1, 44.
4. 1957 QOD, 567-609.
5. *The Desire of Ages,* 49, 117.
6. In fact, almost unbelievably, the Biblical Research Institute opined in 1989 that "the world church has never viewed these subjects [nature of Christ, nature of sin] as essential to salvation nor to the mission of the remnant church. . . . There can be no strong unity within the world church of God's remnant people so long as segments who hold these views agitate them both in North America and overseas divisions. These topics need to be laid aside and not urged upon our people as necessary issues." Cited in *Issues: The Seventh-day Adventist Church and Certain Private Ministries,* Appendix XVI, 238-244. In fact, many pastors and teachers were advised (as well as threatened) not to speak on these subjects.
7. Nam, 246.
8. J. R. Zurcher, *Touched With Our Feelings* (Hagerstown, MD, Review and Herald Publishing Association, 1999), 175.
9. Nam. *op, cit.,*229-239.
10. Nam observed that "Figuhr seems to have been guilty of overstating his case and misleading his readers. While it is true that the manuscript was widely distributed, documentary evidence and later testimonies from those involved in the publication of the book indicate that there was never a resounding and unanimous 'chorus of approval.' . . .It remained essentially the product of a few men." *op cit.,* 280-281.
11. Nam, 98/

12. Ibid., 247.

13. Ibid., 250-256.

14. Ibid., 240.

15. Ibid., 239-245.

16. Ibid.,, 254, 268.

17. Ibid., 255.

18. 1957 QOD, 8.

19. Unruh, *Adventist Heritage,* fourth quarter, 1977.

20. Nam, *op, cit.,*299, 300.

21. Ibid., 316.

22. Ibid.,, 352.

23. Letter to Local Conference Presidents, Central Union Conference, March 24, 1960. In a letter to Figuhr, on the same date, he said that none of the Adventist bookstores in the Central Union would be stocking Martin's book because it would "confuse the faith of man." Both items cited in Nam, *op. cit.,*346, 347..

24. Ibid., 255.

25. Ibid.

♦ FOUR ♦

Time to See the Big Picture

The issue in 1957 was the fatal attempt to meld (1) the limited understanding of the Adventist trio's understanding of what made Adventism work with (2) Augustinian/Calvinism's Sovereignty of God theme. *What could have made all the difference would have been a biblical review of the Great Controversy Theme in contrast to Calvinism's limited understanding of the character of God and the gospel.* The central question for both parties is: What does God plan to accomplish with His Salvation Plan?

Major Issues in the Great Controversy Theme[1]

In a few words, on God's side, the purpose of the Great Controversy Theme is to prove Satan wrong in his charges against God's character and His government.[2] The issue is always planted in God's created soil of Freedom. Before love, there had to be freedom. All created intelligences beginning with the angels, extending throughout the inhabited worlds were endowed with freedom—the freedom to even say No to God's plan for them. In other words, responsibility (ability to-response) was the actionable word—freedom to respond to their Creator, either positively or negatively. Love is an attribute found only in the larger embracing air of freedom. Throughout the biblical story, God was trying to make clear what He planned to accomplish with His salvation plan as He manifested His fairness, love, and trustworthiness through His dealing with, first the Israelites and eventually in the person of Jesus Christ.

On the human side, the purpose of the Great Controversy Theme is to restore in willing men and women the image of Christ, their Maker. To do so, the Holy Spirit's task is to work out of a person's life all that sin has worked in. By God's grace, men and women, regardless of nationality and level of schooling, can be forgiven and transformed into overcomers who hate sin. People that God and the angels can trust with eternal life will inhabit the redeemed world. No rebels will be granted eternal life. The highest motivation for God's loyalist is to honor God, not to merely impress Him.

Therefore, the following principles do follow:

1. The believer's character determines destiny, not merely one's profession of faith.
2. Perfection is a matter of continual moral growth and not a concern for arbitrary goal posts.
3. Christian growth rests on the profound linkage of human will and divine grace—the grace of pardon and the grace of power.

How does this all work out in theological talk?

Soteriology is the study of the plan of salvation. The life and work of Jesus should be one's chief consideration. How one thinks about Jesus directly affects all other biblical studies, especially Eschatology, the study of Last-day Events.

For Calvinists, their Five Points' yardstick controls all aspects of their soteriology. Their understanding of the utter depravity of mankind rests on their notion of original sin and, thus, the companion doctrine that all men and women are born sinners. Their only explanation for the sinfulness of mankind was to simply declare that we all are sinners because Adam sinned. Because of their controlling "sovereignty of God" principle, mankind could not possibly have free will and thus any responsibility. If anyone were to be "saved" it would have to be due to God's sovereign choice, not man's response.

Therefore, for the Calvinist, if Jesus is man's Savior, He would have to die for those that are already elected to be saved. Further, our Lord could not have inherited as we do the genetic stream of His ancestors because, if so, He too would have been born a sinner. The Calvinistic solution: Jesus had to be "exempt" from all inherited tendencies to sin—just as Roman Catholics had concluded. Thus, to make their major premise work, the elect would be those who were "given" faith and thus the "ability" to profess gratefulness for Christ's substitutionary atonement. Because they had been foreordained to be saved, the elect could not fall out of grace; they could never be "unsaved."

Adventist Template and Calvinist Template Incompatible

Obviously, Seventh-day Adventists should have great difficulty trying to harmonize their understanding of salvation with their Calvinist friends, no matter how much linguistic gymnastics they could muster. The problem in 1955-1957 was that foggy thinking on the part of the Adventists led them, almost unknowingly, into capitulating to the Evangelicals. Here began fifty years of focus on some kind of objective atonement without equal weight on the subjective aspect of the atonement that would have highlighted our Lord's work as our High Priest.

The Adventist trio were untrained theologians. They had not seen that 1) the Scriptures embrace a complete system of truth and that every part in the Bible should sustain and not contradict any other part; 2) that any defective or imperfect concept of any one doctrine must inevitably lead to confusion and error throughout the whole system and 3) that two or more self-consistent systems of theology are possible but they cannot both be biblically correct. For instance, it is impossible to join the tectonic plates of Augustianisn-Calvinism with either Pelagianism/SemiPelagianism or Arminian-Adventism. Unless one is prepared for a plethora of troubles

This explains the volcanic eruptions that soon developed.

Obviously, Andreasen and Others Aroused

All this incompatibility aroused Andreasen and many others. The veteran theologian knew from personal study and experience that only those who acknowledge the binding claim of the moral law can explain the nature and purpose, of the atonement—that when Jesus paid the indebtedness of the repentant sinner, He did not give him or her license to continue sinning but to now live responsibly in obedience to the law. Calvinists are not able to process this fundamental thought.

Because Andreasen started with the systematic principle of God's freedom and man's responsibility and not God's sovereignty and man's predestination, the veteran theologian saw immediately that the Adventist tectonic plate should be an unmovable theological mass.

Thus, the ruling principle of human responsibility led Andreasen toward a different understanding of the Atonement. He saw that the sanctuary doctrine (including the purpose of the Old Testament sanctuary service and its New Testament application as best described in the Book of Hebrews) painted a picture of the unbroken union between the objective and subjective aspects of the Atonement. From the moment Christ was "slain from the foundation

of the world" (Revelation 13:8) to the end of the millennium when Satan and the consequences of sin will be no more, Andreasen could see what the Calvinists could not.

Biblical Sanctuary Doctrine[3]

The sanctuary doctrine emphasizes how God forgives and justifies only penitent men or women, but more! The doctrine equally emphasizes that God promises to empower the penitent so that sins are eliminated by the inner graces of the Holy Spirit. The penitent men and women who continue to cooperate with God will truly find the peace, assurance, and divine empowerment that comes in completing the gospel plan in his or her life. This was never made clear to our Calvinist friends in 1957 and it has been one of the causes of Adventist theological muddle in the years since.[4]

Notes:

1. See Appendix A: "Issues in the Great Controversy."
2. "Great and marvelous are Your works, Lord God Almighty! Just and true are Your ways, O King of the saints" (Revelation 15:3). "For true and righteous are His judgments" (Revelation 19:2). For a biblical essay on how the Great Controversy Theme pervades the Scriptures, see the author's "God on trail," in *Ministry,* May 1982. For a extended unfolding of the Great Controversy Theme, see author's *God At Risk* (Roseville, CA: Amazing Facts, 2004), 408 pp.
3. Exegetical methodology, biblical theology, etc., have their limitations for each text, chapter, book, because their drilling for meaning depends on their presuppositions. Each scholar works with his own presupposition as he/she sifts biblical materials. "Only systematic theology provides the tools and disciplinary space for such a task . . . . Biblical theology requires a center from which to gather the vast variety of issues, histories, and teachings present in biblical texts. . . .Thus, the proper expression of the Sanctuary doctrine as hermeneutical vision of a complete and harmonious system of truth requires the contributions of new approaches to biblical and systematic theologies. . . . From this foundational level, the Sanctuary doctrine becomes the hermeneutical light guiding in the interpretation of these far-reaching ideas (hermeneutical conditions of theological method) and in the understanding of the complete and harmonious system of Christian theology." Fernando Canale, "From Vision to System," *Journal of the Adventist Theological Society,* 16/1-2 (2005)
4. Canale is correct in his understanding of the necessity of a central hermeneutical principle for any theological system; for Adventist theology, Canale believes that foundation principle is the sanctuary doctrine. This is precisely what the QOD trio never seemed to understand. Note the following: "The scripture which above all others had been both the foundation and the central pillar of the advent faith, was the declaration, "Unto two thousand and three hundred days; then shall the sanctuary be cleansed (Daniel 8:14)."—White, *The Great Controversy,* 409. "The subject of the sanctuary was the key with unlocked the mystery of the disappointment of 1844. It opened to view a

complete system of truth, connected and harmonious," Ibid., 423. "Those who received the light concerning the sanctuary and the immutability of the law of God, were filled with joy and wonder, as they saw the beauty and harmony of the system of truth that opened to their understanding." Ibid., 454.

♦ FIVE ♦

What Happens When Theological Clarity Becomes Fog?

In the years since 1957, both clergy and laypeople have experienced this theological and leadership muddle. Think of how many articles in Adventist periodicals have argued over whether sanctification was even part of righteousness by faith. Think of how many churches were rent over those who said justification was far more important than sanctification. Behind all this was confusion over what happened on the Cross—and what happened in 1957.

Further, how many pastors left the Adventist Church because they were convinced by very persuasive scholars that Christ in the Heavenly Sanctuary was not only *not* needed, but a twisted fabrication of Ellen White's theology? How many young people were relieved if not elated to hear that their character had nothing to do with their salvation? Or that Jesus paid it all on the Cross, and our only responsibility was to accept His death as full payment and not to worry about doing anything to add to what Jesus did for us? All this is pure confusion!

180-degree Turn on the Nature of Christ's Humanity

The other chief concern that Andreasen and others had with QOD was

the astonishing, 180-degree deflection regarding the nature of Christ's humanity, in addition to the murky explanation of the Adventist understanding of the atonement.

Two Trigger Words

Along with the lack of careful biblical scholarship and the general misuse of Ellen White quotes, two words became flaming beacons that something was terribly confused. Those words were *exempt* and *vicarious*—words that had been most used by the Roman Catholic Church, as well as many Protestants, to explain their novel understanding of the human Jesus.

QOD states that Jesus was "exempt from the inherited passions and pollutions that corrupt the natural descendants of Adam."[1] Further, we read, "Jesus took, all that He *bore,* whether the burden and penalty of our iniquities, or the diseases and frailties of our human nature—all was taken and borne *vicariously*" (emphasis in text).[2]

What should we make of these interesting words? Why did these words add to the Grand Canyon between classic Adventism and Calvinism?

These two words, *exempt* and *vicariously,* pleased our Calvinist friends because of their "Points" that emphasized (1) that men and women are not responsible for their sins, because they are born sinful and (2) are "saved" only because God so elects them. Thus, as applied to Jesus, since all men are corrupt from birth, Christ could not have come as all babies do, accepting the genetic flow of His forebears (or He would have needed a Savior as well). Therefore, for salvation purposes, He must be seen as our Substitute only. As our Example, He would only be an inspiration, a portrait of a better life that is unreachable this side of the grave.

These two words, *exempt* and *vicariously,* really turned on Andreasen's afterburners.

Though Jesus could vicariously die for our sins, how could His human life of 33 years relate to our salvation vicariously? He made it possible that we will not be punished for our sins—He died *for* us, vicariously. But how could He live as our Example vicariously? Does that mean we don't have to live an overcoming life, resisting the tempter at every turn—because He did it for us vicariously? Did He keep the law for us vicariously? Rather, in resisting evil as our Example, He showed us how to "walk as He walked" (1 John 2:6). Although He died for us *vicariously,* He didn't obey for us *vicariously*! Vicariously, He gave us freedom from the "wages of sin."

Another Sub-heading Flaw

But this theological confusion was heightened by another flawed sub-heading in the compilation of Ellen White quotations: "VI. Bore the Imputed Sin and Guilt of the World."[3] Calvinists would love this statement, but not a trained Adventist thinker! Not one of the listed White statements came close to the implication of this heading! White couldn't have supported Christ bearing our "imputed sin and guilt" because her understanding of the Bible overruled such Calvinistic representations. Similarly, she never associated "pollution" with "passion" is if the two concepts were interchangeable.[4]

The next step follows logically: If Christ had such an advantage over all men and women, it would be unfair, and even unreasonable, for God to expect us to live and overcome as He did (Revelation 3:21). Thus, for Calvinists, God could not expect us to "stop sinning." Further, with this reasoning, we are told that He saves us "in" our sins, not "from" our sins (Matt. 1:21).

It should not require a rocket scientist to see the deep gulf between this understanding of salvation and the century-old, classic Adventist understanding. However, the nuclear fallout of the 1957 QOD provided the climate for this kind of thinking to become standard fare in many seminary classes and later, in many of our college religion departments. Of course, it was challenged by others, but they were classed as theological dinosaurs.

For anyone thinking that the QOD trio had it right in stating that only a "lunatic fringe" had believed that (1) Jesus took our sinful nature (but not a sinning nature) and that (2) His "temptations" to sin were exactly like what other human beings have to face and therefore could have sinned—all they had to do was read, for one example, Francis D. Nichol's two *Review* editorials on July 10 and 17, 1952.

Nichol's Editorials

Nichol, invited to become an associate editor of the *Review and Herald* in 1927, was elected editor-in-chief in 1945. In part he said in his July 10 editorial: "Indeed, just what is comprehended by the term 'sinful nature'? Protestants, from the earliest of Reformation times, have been unable to agree. But certain critics of the Advent Movement seemingly have no difficulty whatever in the whole matter, and move forward with dogmatic assurance through the mystery of the nature of Christ and the mystery of a sinful nature to the conclusion that Seventh-day Adventists are guilty of fearful heresy. . . .In our literature that could be considered as truly

authoritative on this is what Mrs. E. G. White has written. . . . On page 49 [of *The Desire of Ages*] Mrs. White declares: 'Into the world where Satan claimed dominion God permitted His Son to come, a helpless babe, subject to the weakness of humanity. He permitted Him to meet life's peril in common with every human soul, to fight the battle as every child of humanity must fight it, at the risk of failure and eternal loss.'

"This is Adventist belief. And we hold this belief because we feel it agrees with revelation and reason." Nichol then proceeded to quote New Testament verses and a lengthy excerpt from F. W. Farrar's *Life of Christ,* after which he wrote: "These should suffice to prove that the Adventist view of Christ in relation to temptation is not a strange, heretical teaching. . . . When we speak of the taint of sin, the germs of sin, we should remember that we are using metaphorical language. Critics, especially those who see the Scriptures through Calvinistic eyes, read into the term 'sinful flesh' something that Adventist theology does not require."

In his July 17 editorial, he quoted numerous theologians who also declared that "Christ, the 'last Adam,' won the battle with the tempter; and we, through His promised forgiveness and power, may also win. Adam could have won, but he lost. Christ could have lost, but He won. Therein lies the startling contrast. and the contrast is heightened by the fact that Christ was born into the human family some four thousand years after sin's entry into our world, with all that is mysteriously involved of a weakening of body and mind in the fight against sin. . . . Christ won despite the fact that He took on Himself 'the likeness of sinful flesh,' with all that that implies of the baleful and weakening effect of sin on the body and nervous system of man, and its evil effects on his environment.

"The objector feels that the only way to do honor to Christ and to protect Him from all taint of sin is to take the position that He could not sin. But what comfort and assurance of personal victory over sin can we find in a spotless Christ if His freedom from sin as He walked this earth was not truly a victory over temptation but an inability to sin? We would rightly stand in awe of such a Holy Being. But we could not see in Him one who was 'made like unto his brethren' 'in all things,' one who being 'tempted like as we are' 'is able to succour' us when we are 'tempted.'"

Brief Review of a Hundred Years

The fascinating part of this brief review of Adventist history is that between the years 1852–1952 we find more than 1,200 similar statements (as highlighted by Nichol) that Christ's human nature was fallen like ours and not like that of the unfallen Adam. Four hundred of these statements were written and published by Ellen G. White. In addition during this 100-year

period, thousands of statements written and published by Ellen White and other Adventist authors emphasized that by the power of the Holy Spirit, Christians can stop sinning even as Jesus could overcome.[5] *Nichol was simply part of the historical stream of classic Adventist thought.*

Branson's 1954 Book

But there was more that the QOD trio should have been reading. Unfortunately, in 1954, W H. Branson, president of the General Conference, retired for health reasons. Author of many books in addition to valiant service in China, he finished his last book, *Drama of the Ages,* just months prior to his retirement. He wrote: "Here is a glorious truth, a marvelous condescension; for God the Son deigned to dwell with men even to the point of taking upon Himself sinful flesh and becoming a member of the human family. . . .The Catholic doctrine of the 'immaculate conception' is that Mary, the mother of our Lord, was preserved from original sin. If this be true, then Jesus did not partake of man's sinful nature. This belief cuts off the lower rungs of the ladder, and leaves man without a Saviour who can be touched with the feeling of man's infirmities, and who can sympathize with them."[6]

Then Branson explained why Christ took the fallen nature of humanity: "In order for Christ to understand the weakness of human nature, He had to experience it. In order for Him to be sympathetic with men in their trials, He also had to be tried. He must suffer hunger, weariness, disappointment, sorrow, and persecution. He must tread the same paths, live under the same circumstances, and die the same death. Therefore He became bone of our bone and flesh of our flesh, His Incarnation was in actual humanity."[7]

It has been well said that if Branson had continued his presidency, QOD would never have seen the light of day!

Strange Act of 1949

Except! Except for that strange act in 1949 that set the stage for the overture that would soon present the strange music in the new opera called QOD! It was the first of many acts to come.

The issue? Since 1915, Adventists had published *Bible Readings for the Home Circle.* Exceptionally large numbers had been sold in several countries. Many thousands became Adventists after reading this powerful book. Here is the original question and answer on the humanity of Christ *before* the editing in 1949:

> "How fully did Christ share our common humanity? 'Wherefore in *all things it behooved him to be made like unto his brethren,* that he might

be a merciful and faithful high priest in things pertaining to God, to make reconciliation for the sins of the people.' Hebrews 2:17. Note.—In His humanity Christ partook of our sinful, fallen nature. If not, then He was not 'made like unto His brethren,' was not 'in all points tempted like as we are' (Hebrews 4:15), did not overcome as we have to overcome, and is not, therefore the complete and perfect Saviour man needs and must have to be saved. The idea that Christ was born of an immaculate or sinless mother, inherited no tendencies to sin, and for this reason did not sin, removes Him from the realm of a fallen world, and from the very place where help is needed. On His human side, Christ inherited just what every child of Adam inherits—a sinful nature. On the divine side, from His very conception He was begotten and born of the Spirit. And all this was done to place mankind on vantage ground, and to demonstrate that *in the same way* every one who is 'born of the Spirit' may gain like victories over sin in his own sinful flesh. Thus each one is to overcome *as Christ overcame.* Revelation 3:21. Without this birth there can be no victory over temptation, and no salvation from sin. John 3:3–7" (Emphasis in the original).[8]

Now follows the 1949 revision:

"How fully did Christ share our common humanity? '*Wherefore in all things it behoved Him to be made like His brethren,* that He might be a merciful and faithful high priest in things pertaining to God, to make reconciliation for the sins of the people.' Verse 17.

"Note—Jesus Christ is both Son of God and Son of man. As a member of the human family 'it behoved Him to be made like unto His brethren'—'in the likeness of sinful flesh.' Just how far that 'likeness' goes is a mystery of the incarnation, which men have never been able to solve. The Bible clearly teaches that Christ was tempted just as other men are tempted—'in all points . . . like as we are.' Such temptation must necessarily include the possibility of sinning; but Christ was without sin. There is no Bible support for the teaching that the mother of Christ, by an immaculate conception, was cut off from the sinful inheritance of the race, and therefore her divine Son was incapable of sinning. Concerning this false doctrine, Dean F. W. Farrar has well said: 'Some, in a zeal at once intemperate and ignorant, have claimed for Him not only an actual sinlessness but a nature to which sin was divinely and miraculously impossible. What then? If His great conflict were a mere deceptive phantasmagoria, how can the narrative of it profit us? If *we* have to fight the battle clad in the armor of human free-will, . . . what comfort is it to us if our great Captain fought not only victoriously, but without real danger; not only uninjured, but without even the possibility of a wound. . . . Let us beware of contradicting the express teaching of the Scriptures,. . . by a supposition that He was not liable to real temptation.'—*The Life of Christ* (1883 ed.), vol. 1, p. 57.

God's Demonstration of Victory

"Where did God, in Christ, condemn sin, and gain the victory for us over temptation and sin?

'For what the law could not do, in that it was weak through the flesh, God sending His own Son in the likeness of sinful flesh, and for sin, *condemned sin in the flesh.*" Romans 8:3.

"Note—God, in Christ, condemned sin, not by pronouncing against it merely as a judge sitting on the judgment seat, but by coming and living *in the flesh,* and yet without sinning. In Christ, He demonstrated that it is possible, by His grace and power to resist temptation, overcome sin, and *live a sinless life in the flesh.*"

In 1956, this *revised* question/answer passage in *Bible Readings for the Home Circle* first became public knowledge in Anderson's *Ministry* September editorial. He used this revision as an example of Adventist literature that had been purged. No one apparently had seen the edited *Bible Readings* before this September editorial. Anderson's editorial hit the fan!

Anderson's Explanation

Here is how Anderson explained the revision: "Many years ago a statement appeared in *Bible Readings for the Home Circle* (1915 edition) which declared that Christ came 'in sinful flesh.' Just how this expression slipped into the book is difficult to know. It has been quoted many times by critics, and all around the world, as being typical of Adventist Christology. But when that book was revised in 1949 this expression was eliminated, since it was recognized as being out of harmony with our true position."[9]

However, when we look at the original 1915 statement, it is obvious that the phrase "in sinful flesh" was not an "expression" (it took almost a full page of explanation so that no reader should have been confused). Further, this nearly full page of explanation of "sinful flesh" was certainly not "out of harmony with our true position." It was clearly harmonious with the position of dozens of Adventist writers as well as with hundreds of Ellen White statements that were the most lucid on the subject.[10]

The question should have been obvious to the QOD trio, even in reading the 1949 revision: How could our Lord condemn sin in the flesh (Romans 8:3, 4) if He did not take "sinful flesh"?

What was causing this blind spot in the QOD trio's theological response to the Evangelical's concern? In the attempt to appear gracious and accommodating, they read into the expression, "fallen, sinful nature," the "corruptions" that come from actually choosing to sin. (Publishing house editors, Sabbath School lesson editors, many leaders, and Ellen White for scores of years—had differentiated between inherited tendencies and cultivated habits of sin.) But with this desire to please the Evangelicals, the QOD trio allowed their visiting friends to set the agenda. What seems more than interesting is that the revision did not mute the Adventist understanding of

how Christ's life and death made it possible for faithful Christians "*to live a sinless life in sinful flesh.*"

In a way, I find this little episode that started a theological forest fire, amusing, except the QOD/Evangelical dialogue kept missing the whole point of what God wants to accomplish in His Plan of Salvation.

Scholarly Fraud

But there was more in this September 1956 issue of *Ministry*. Here for the first time were fragments from Ellen White's writings that Dr. Knight has shown to be far off the mark of careful scholarship—excerpts contrary to context and ellipses that amounted to scholarly fraud. And this was the same set of quotations later found in Appendix B of QOD and the last section of Volume 7A in the *Seventh-day Adventist Bible Commentary*! The *Commentary* editors knew nothing about this later inclusion.

Anderson's editorial (mentioned above) recommended this compilation "as full coverage of this subject as can be found in the writings of Ellen G. White. . . . As far as we have been able to discover, this compilation fully represents the thinking of the messenger of the Lord on this question. A few other statements have been found, but these are either repetitions or mere verbal variations, and add no new thought." Amazing!

Further, in the editorial, we find: "In only three or four places in all these inspired counsels have we founds such expressions as 'fallen nature' and 'sinful nature.' But these are strongly counterbalanced and clearly explained by many other statements that reveal the thought of the writer. Christ did indeed partake of our *nature*, our *human nature* with all its physical limitations, but not of our *carnal* nature with all its lustful corruptions" (emphasis in the editorial).

Anderson's Straw Man

Let's take a little time out to analyze again what my friend Anderson is saying. In logic theory, he here is using the "straw man" to throw off or mislead his opponents: *no Adventist has ever applied the words "corrupt, carnal, or lustful" to our Savior! Never!* Because of Anderson's marvelous record as an evangelist and editor of *Ministry*, his readers blithely accepted his manufactured comments without a pause for further reflection.

But we should now pause a moment and at least look briefly at the seventy-year writing ministry of Ellen White. Definitely, she referred to our Lord's humanity as possessing "our sinful nature." She always put this profound concept in connection with what it meant to our individual

salvation: "The example He has left must be followed. He took upon His sinless nature *our sinful nature* that He might know how to succor those that are tempted" (emphasis supplied).[11]

Again, "Clad in the vestments of humanity, the Son of God came down to the level of those he wished to save. In him was no guile or sinfulness; he was ever pure and undefiled; yet he took upon him *our sinful nature*. Clothing his divinity with humanity, that he might associate with fallen humanity, he sought to redeem for man that which by disobedience Adam had lost, for himself and for the world" (emphasis supplied).[12]

This particular White quotation reminds us of Gregory of Naziansus (329–ca. 389) who said: "For that which He has not assumed He has not healed; but that which is united to His Godhead is also saved,:[13] Gregory was a leading theologian who helped to settle the Arian controversy as well as the teachings of Apollinarius, who denied the rational soul in Christ and held that the body of Jesus came from heaven.

Ellen White Consistency

Many times Ellen White quoted Romans 8:3, 4 to signal this weighty concept: "'For what the law could not do, in that it was weak through the flesh'—it could not justify man, because in his *sinful nature* he could not keep the law—'God sending His own Son in the likeness of sinful flesh, and for sin, condemned sin in the flesh: that the righteousness of the law might be fulfilled in us, who walk not after the flesh, but after the Spirit.' Romans 5:1, 3:31, 8:3, 4" (emphasis supplied).[14]

Briefly, it would take many pages in this review to list the quotes of her constant theme that Jesus came into this world to accept "the results of the working of the great law of heredity. What these results were is shown in the history of His earthly ancestors. He came with such a heredity to share our sorrows and temptations, and to give us the example of a sinless life. . . . Yet into the world where Satan claimed dominion God permitted His Son to come, a helpless babe, subject to the weakness of humanity. He permitted Him to meet life's peril in common with every human soul, to fight the battle as every child of humanity must fight it, at the risk of failure and eternal loss."[15]

Obviously, if the QOD trio emphasized even slightly the mass of Ellen White quotes that linked our Lord's humanity with fallen mankind, Martin and Barnhouse would have quickly packed their bags and continued their attacks on the Adventists as cultists, in their eyes. As Calvinists, they had no other choice.

Not a Mere Theological Exercise

But Ellen White did not emphasize our Lord's humanity as a mere theological exercise. She virtually always linked His humanity with mankind's only hope for rescue from the cords of sin. In other words, theologically speaking, what one thinks about the humanity of Christ directly affects what one thinks about what our Lord expects from men and women regarding character transformation. Further, this linkage is exactly what Andreasen saw that the QOD trio did not—that character transformation had much to do with the Adventist understanding of Revelation 14 and thus the Second Advent.[16] And they knew that if they emphasized this linkage, it would have demolished the Five Points of Calvinism.

For example: "He for our sakes laid aside His royal robe, stepped down from the throne in heaven, and condescended to clothe His divinity with humility, and became like one of us except in sin, that His life and character should be a pattern for all to copy, that they might have the precious gift of eternal life."[17]

These insights could be reproduced hundreds of times: "The character of the Lord Jesus Christ is to be reproduced in those who believe in him as their personal Saviour. They will be 'rich in good works, ready to distribute, willing to communicate; laying up in store for themselves a good foundation against the time to come, that they may lay hold on eternal life.' Our acceptance with God is not upon the ground of our good works, but our reward will be according to our works. 'For what the law could not do, in that it was weak through the flesh, God sending his own Son in the likeness of sinful flesh, and for sin, condemned sin in the flesh; that the righteousness of the law might be fulfilled in us, who walk not after the flesh, but after the Spirit.'"[18]

Another *Ministry* editorial

But another *Ministry* editorial turned up the heat for blastoff. *Before* the publication of QOD in September, *after* the Calvinistic leaders had accepted the answers provided by the QOD trio, in April 1957, Louise Kleuser, associate secretary of the General Conference Ministerial Association, and a graceful, lifelong Bible Worker, wrote that the soon-to-be published QOD was "a new milestone" in the history of the Adventist church. More kerosene on the fire!

Some would call these *Ministry* editorials and articles supporting QOD a gigantic fraud that would be chiseled into Adventist history. If not a fraud, it would be at least gross misrepresentation!

Strange Hermeneutics

One of the strangest techniques ever used in Adventist literature was the use of a personal letter as if in that one letter Ellen White was changing seventy years of her teaching ministry. As if that one letter indeed said something (which I doubt) that "counterbalanced" the many lucid, unequivocal statements in just one book, *The Desire of Ages,* never mind hundreds of other statements elsewhere, like those in *Desire.* That really is a test of one's hermeneutical principles!

Instead of using Ellen White's hundreds of similar thoughts to help us to understand certain phrases in the Baker letter, the QOD trio used the Baker letter to explain what White meant in hundreds of her unambiguous statements about the humanity of Jesus! For the purposes of this study, we can safely say that the Baker letter can be understood and reconciled with all of White's hundreds of statements as well as biblical exegesis.[19] Ellen White does not have a wax nose, as some have suggested!

Misrepresentation Worked Both Ways

Of course, the misrepresentation worked both ways: Calvinists were to be convinced that Adventists had changed their teachings and Adventists had to be convinced that we had not changed our teachings. It worked, for awhile! For forty-five years, secrecy even veiled the names of the QOD trio, except for those of us who were "there" when it was happening.

How do we explain all this? If both parties had stood back for even two weeks and as trained scholars reviewed their data, their quotations, etc., they would have suddenly seen that they were proposing and accepting garbled references and conclusions without adequate verification. No graduate student in any university could have even earned a master's degree with such substandard scholarship! Yet, I have read several doctoral dissertations that have defended the inconsistencies and underwhelming logic of QOD.

Dr. Jean Zurcher, an Adventist scholar and distinguished administrator, was well recognized in the academic world for his notable book, *The Nature and Destiny of Man.* In 1999, he wrote *Touched With Our Feelings*—one of the most persuasive books ever written aimed at putting the record straight regarding the QOD nuclear bomb. He reviewed a century of Adventist thinking regarding the divine and human nature of Christ, including many extracts from official church publications on two continents. Further, he examined the printed material since 1957 that extolled QOD, all in lockstep, naive acceptance.

In all his broad research, Zurcher found no sign of any disagreement among Seventh-day Adventists anywhere, on both continents, regarding the human nature of Christ, before the middle 1950s. He used the words, "remarkable unanimity" to sum up his research regarding pre-QOD Adventist thinking on the humanity of Christ.[20]

An Attempted Compromise

I know some are wondering how later administrators and theological leaders eventually attempted a compromise that would quiet opposition to QOD. Some suggested an alternative or a third option that would explain what seemed to them to be contradictory statements in the writings of Ellen White. It was a brave attempt at a mediating position between the pre-lapsarians and the post-lapsarians.

It worked like this: 1) Christ's humanity was not Adam's innocent humanity before his Fall; that is, He inherited the weaknesses of our "innocent infirmities" such as hunger, pain, sorrow, and death. 2) He came only in the "likeness of sinful flesh" (Romans 8:3); that is, He did not inherit a "tendency to sin" or "sinful propensities."

How shall we relate to this compromise, the recent third option in the Adventist Christological debate? First, we should note that Jesus did not come to liberate humanity from our "innocent infirmities" but to deliver from indwelling sin. That is why Jesus came "in the likeness [not unlikeness] of sinful flesh" (Romans 8:3) and "in all things He had to be made like unto his brethren" (Hebrews 2:17).

Further, we must recognize the difference between "inherent propensities" and "evil propensities." In Ellen White's world, these two phrases do not say the same thing. A propensity is a tendency, a bent, an enticement to temptation. If resisted, it is not sin (James 4:17; John 9:49; 15:22). "Inherent propensities" become "evil" or "sinful propensities" only after yielding to temptation.[21]

The same distinction may be made between "evil tendencies" and "evil propensities." Jesus never had "evil propensities." But Ellen White wrote that Jesus met and was "subjected to all the evil tendencies to which man is heir working in every conceivable manner to destroy his faith."[22]

Henry Melvill

Probably the strongest argument (and strangest) that the third option makes is the connection they see between some phraseology Ellen White may have borrowed from a sermon by Henry Melvill.[23] Melvill taught that *fallen* human nature had two characteristics: innocent infirmities and

sinful propensities—Jesus took the first but not the second. Melvill said that before the Fall, Adam had neither. But Jesus, weakened by four thousand years of sin, Melvill said, assumed mankind's "innocent infirmities" but not the "sinful propensities." Nice try, but Melvill was burdened with his Calvinistic presuppositions!

Ellen White also borrowed phrases from Octavius Winslow's *The Glory of the Redeemer,*[24] who also used language, similar to Melvill, in describing Christ's humanity. Some Adventists, unfortunately, leaped immediately into thinking that a few words from Melvill and Winslow would help us understand what Ellen White meant in the scores of times she used similar words.

Strange reasoning! Perhaps it would have been better hermeneutics to turn the reasoning around: read Ellen White to help us to understand what she was warning Baker[25] about and what Melvill "should" have written to be more exegetically correct.

Observations come to mind immediately: 1) Ellen White never used the phrase, "innocent infirmities." 2) She used "infirmities" in the sense that "for four thousand years the race had been decreasing in physical strength, in mental power, and in moral worth; and Christ took upon Him the *infirmities of degenerate humanity*. Only thus could He rescue man from the lowest depths of his degradation. . . . Our Saviour took humanity, with all its liabilities" {emphasis supplied).[26]

Further, we think it would have been helpful for the *Annotated Edition of QOD* to include Ellen White's many insights, such as "Christ's perfect humanity is the same that man may have through connection with Christ . . . .Christ took our nature, fallen but not corrupted, and would not be corrupted unless He received the words of Satan in the place of the words of God."[27]

Or, make reference to White's understanding regarding how Jesus was saved from corruption by His godly mother and their leaning together on the empowerment of the Holy Spirit:

> "Jesus knows the burden of every mother's heart. . . . Let mothers come to Jesus with their perplexities. They will find grace sufficient to aid them in the management of their children. . . .. Even the babe in its mother's arms may dwell as under the shadow of the Almighty through the faith of the praying mother. John the Baptist was filled with the Holy Spirit from his birth. If we will live in communion with God, we too may expect the divine Spirit to mold our little ones, even from their earliest moments."[28]

In other words, whenever Ellen White applied the term "corrupt

propensities" to Jesus she meant that Jesus never sinned, never corrupted Himself. Whenever Ellen said anything similar to the following quotation, she never thought in terms of "vicariously": "Christ bore the sins and infirmities of the race as they existed when He came to the earth to help men. In behalf of the race, with the weaknesses of fallen man upon Him, He was to stand the temptations of Satan upon all points wherewith man would be assailed."[29]

Melvill's Federal Theology

Henry Melvill was a federalist; much of his Christology and salvation theory can then be better understood under his federalistic rubric: "If a man be a fallen man, he must have fallen in Adam [the natural/federal head of the human race]; in other words, he must be one of those whom Adam federally represented. But Christ, as being emphatically the seed of the woman, was not thus federally represented; and therefore Christ fell not, as we fall in Adam. He had not been a party to the broken covenant, and thus could not be a sharer in the guilt consequences of the infraction."[30]

Federal theology, often called "Covenant Theology," is rooted in Augustinian theology that began with Augustine's notion that all mankind is inherently depraved and sinful *because* we all sinned in Adam. Further, in Federalism theology, God holds *all mankind* responsible for the violation of a covenant that God made with Adam although all descendants of Adam had no part in its violation. Common sense should tell us that imputation of sin cannot precede and thus account for corruption; corruption is the result of a choice to sin, not the cause of it. One can do wonders with theological gymnastics!

Because of this Federal or Covenant Theology, Calvinist thinkers, including Melvill and Winslow, are blind to their Augustinian roots. Whenever they use the word "corrupt" or "corruption," especially when discussing the humanity of Christ, they must be understood as employing the sovereignty of God notion that required more theological gymnastics to explain why we are sinners! Their chief texts are Romans 5:17–19 and 1 Corinthians 15:22. Thus, in their interpretation: "as the sin of Adam was legally and effectively *our* sin so the obedience of Christ is legally and effectively the righteousness of all believers. . . . To provide their salvation [those federally related to Adam], the needed reparation had to made by another who was not of federal connection with Adam and thus was free from the imputation of guilt. Federal theology represented these requirements as being met in Christ, the second Adam, in whom a new race begins."[31]

Ellen White, no Calvinist

Ellen White did not buy into this kind of reasoning, which kept her from using Melvill's formulation of a "third" way of looking at the humanity of Christ. Of course, we find a voracious reader like Ellen White indebted to phrases of others, such as D'Aubigne, Wylie, Melvill, Winslow, and Hanna, etc.—phrases that spelled out her desired concepts more eloquently than her own choice of words in her hurry to complete a manuscript. The choice phrases did not alter Ellen White's thought intent but did make her meaning more pleasing and forceful. She borrowed some of their felicitous phrases but not their theological intent. Ellen knew when to distinguish truth from error whenever she gleaned helpful thoughts from others.[32]

Adventists Not Alone

Before leaving our comments on the nature of Christ issue it would be salutary to note that Adventists are not alone in their 150 years of understanding the humanity of Christ. Many biblical scholars have challenged the so-called "orthodox" view that Christ somehow took Adam's pre-Fall nature rather than the human equipment inherited by every other child of Adam. Among these are, and not limited to, Edward Irving, Thomas Erskine, Herman Kohlbrugge, Eduard Bohl, Karl Barth, T. F. Torrrance, Nels Ferré, C. E. B. Cranfield, Harold Roberts, Lesslie Newbigin, E. Stauffer, Anders Nygren, C. K. Barrett, Wolfhard Pannenberg, and Eric Baker, among many more.[33]

Would Barnhouse and Martin include this galaxy as the "lunatic fringe" of the Protestant world?

Andreasen's Second Concern

The other major concern of Andreasen and others looking on from the sidelines was QOD's less-than-lucid language used to describe the Adventist doctrines of the atonement, sanctuary service (type and antitype), and the investigative judgment.

Froom's February 1957 article in *Ministry* entitled "The Priestly Application of the Atoning Act" was designed to prepare readers for QOD, yet to be published. He continued his typical cherry-picking of Ellen White statements. However, in this article, Froom rightly wrote, on one hand, that the atonement could not be limited to Christ's death on the cross or the investigative judgment in heaven, that the atonement "clearly embraces both—one aspect being incomplete without the other, and each being the indispensable complement of the other." All right, so far!

But, on the other hand, he used unfortunate language to describe that Christ's death provided "a complete, perfect, and final atonement for man's sin" and "a completed act of atonement." Because of these poorly chosen words, Andreasen felt that Froom had swung too closely to the Calvinist viewpoint in over-emphasizing the Cross at the expense of other equally important sanctuary truths.

Later, after Andreasen's agitation (which I think was overstated on this occasion) aroused many others around the country, Figuhr himself felt that "it would have been better if that article of Brother Froom's had not appeared in *The Ministry*."[34]

All this before QOD had been printed! As I see it, *if* the QOD trio were wise and secure in their opinions, they would have circulated their manuscript pages to Andreasen, as they did to many others. If they had, some of Andreasen's concerns would have been eliminated. He would have seen on pages 342–347 that QOD did indeed present a "wider connotation" when discussing the atonement. That is, they fully agreed "that the work accomplished on Calvary involves also the "application" of the atoning sacrifice of Christ to the seeking soul. This is provided for in the priestly ministry of our blessed Lord, our great High Priest in the sanctuary above."[35] Good—but they were not finished.

Further, QOD correctly showed their Arminian understanding of the atonement on 1957 QOD, p. 350: "But this sacrificial work will actually benefit human hearts *only* as we surrender our lives to God and experience the miracle of the new birth. In this experience Jesus our High Priest *applies to us the benefits* of His atoning sacrifice" (emphasis in text).

QOD Trio's Defense to Andreasen's Charges

What was the trio's proof? They quoted *Early Writings,* page 260: "The great Sacrifice had been offered and had been accepted, and the Holy Spirit which descended on the day of Pentecost carried the minds of the disciples from the earthly sanctuary to the heavenly, where Jesus had entered by His own blood, to shed upon His disciples the *benefits* of His atonement" (emphasis supplied).

But what is this sentence saying, and what is the context of this cherry-picked sentence?

First, it was in answer to Martin's question 29: "Seventh-day Adventists have frequently been charged with teaching that the atonement was not completed on the cross. Is this charge true?"[36]

How should the Adventist trio have answered this question? For

clarity's sake, they should have replied, "Yes." And then proceeded to explain the larger view of the atonement that a Calvinist would never have thought of. Of course, our Lord's *sacrificial* atonement was completed on the cross, but there is more to be said. The Bible and Ellen White, expanding on the biblical understanding, should robustly have been used to show that the Cross and the heavenly sanctuary are two phases of the Atonement and that the cleansing of the planet from the instigator and consequences of sin completed the Atonement.

Let's look again at *Early Writings* (1851), p. 260. At first glance, the inference is that whatever is going on in the heavenly sanctuary is not part of the atonement but only an "application of the atonement."

The *larger context* of this "benefits of the atonement" statement begins on page 251 of *Early Writings:* "Jesus sent His angels to direct the minds of the disappointed Adventist Millerities to the most holy place, where He had gone to cleanse the sanctuary and make a *special atonement* for Israel" (emphasis supplied).

Then, page 253: "As the priest entered the most holy once a year to cleanse the earthly sanctuary, so Jesus entered the most holy of the heavenly, at the end of the 2300 days of Daniel 8, in 1844, to make a *final atonement* for all who could be benefited by His mediation, and thus to cleanse the sanctuary" (emphasis supplied).[37]

Finally, page 254: "The third angel closes his message thus: 'Here is the patience of the saints: here are they that keep the commandments of God, and the faith of Jesus.' As he repeated these words, he pointed to the heavenly sanctuary. The minds of all who embrace this message are directed to the most holy place, where Jesus stands before the ark, making His *final intercession* for all those for whom mercy still lingers and for those who have ignorantly broken the law of God. This *atonement* is made for the righteous dead as well as for the righteous living. It includes all who died trusting in Christ, but who, not having received the light upon God's commandments, had sinned ignorantly in transgressing its precepts" (emphasis supplied).

Misapplication of One Statement

It is more than difficult to extract from these statements that the Atonement was made at the Cross only and that only its "benefits" summed up Christ's work as High Priest. With a misapplication of one statement taken out of context that inferred that the atonement was completed at the Cross, the Protestant world was satisfied— but the Adventist world was confused and sadly misrepresented.

What seemed even worse, for some strange reason, other than a temporary blindness, the QOD trio did not follow the maturing of Ellen White's larger view of the atonement, subsequent to 1851. If so, Andreasen would have been their loudest cheerleader![38]

For instance, they could have quoted: "It is those who by faith follow Jesus in the great work of the atonement, who received the *benefits* of his mediation in their behalf. . . . They saw that their great High Priest had entered upon another work of ministration , and following Him by faith, they were led to see also the closing work of the church" (emphasis supplied).[39]

The Larger View

What were these High Priestly benefits? As High Priest, "Christ was to complete His work and fulfill His pledge to 'make a man more precious than fine gold; even a man than the golden wedge of Ophir.' Isa. 13:12. All power in heaven and on earth was given to the Prince of life, and He returned to His followers in a world of sin, that He might impart to them of His power and glory."[40]

The QOD trio could have included White's larger view of the atonement:

> "The Spirit was to be given as a regenerating agent, and without this the sacrifice of Christ would have been of no avail. . . . Sin could be resisted and overcome only through the mighty energy of the Third Person of the Godhead, who would come with no modified energy, but in the fullness of divine power. It is the Spirit that makes effectual what has been wrought out by the world's Redeemer. . . . Christ has given His Spirit as a divine power to overcome all hereditary and cultivated tendencies to evil, and to impress His own character upon His church."[41]

These two statements in *The Desire of Ages* are examples of many more that spell out Ellen White's grasp of the ellipse of truth that grounded her mature theology.

But there is so much more where Ellen White had enlarged on this concept of "benefits" and "atonement":

> "And as the typical cleansing of the earthly was accomplished by the removal of the sins by which it had been polluted, so the actual cleansing of the heavenly is to be accomplished by the removal, or blotting out, of the sins which are there recorded. But before this can be accomplished, there must be an examination of the books of record to determine who, through repentance of sin and faith in Christ, are entitled to the *benefits of His atonement*. The cleansing of the sanctuary therefore involves a work of investigation—a work of judgment. This work must be

performed prior to the coming of Christ to redeem His people; for when He comes, His reward is with Him to give to every man according to his works. (Rev. 22:12). . . .

"Attended by heavenly angels, our great High Priest enters the holy of holies and there appears in the presence of God to engage in the last acts of His ministration in behalf of man—to perform the work of investigative judgment and to make an *atonement* for all who are shown to be *entitled to its benefits*. . . . So in the great day of *final atonement* and investigative judgment, the only cases considered are those of the professed people of God [that is, all those of all the ages who professed loyalty to God]" (emphasis supplied).[42]

Notes:

1. QOD, 383.
2. Ibid., 61, 62. It is more than interesting that these two words, *exempt* and *vicariously,* do not appear in the prepublication manuscript copy of QOD. In fact, considerable editing is evident in the section "The Incarnation and the Son of Man," between the prepublication manuscript and the printed book. In some respects, the printed QOD was improved over the manuscript in rhetorical smoothness and clarity of explanation; in other instances, some of the reasons for Andreasen's concerns were greatly augmented. At this point in time, I cannot determine when and where the editorial staff of the Review and Herald Publishing Association ended their editing at the request of the General Conference officers, as prompted by the QOD trio. See also Nam, *op. cit.* 99.
3. See Appendix B: "Ellen White's Use of Words Such as Passions, Inclinations, Propensities, Corruptions, etc."
4. We are indebted to Ralph Larson for marshaling these statements in *The Word Was Made Flesh* (Cherry Valley, CA: The Cherrystone Press, 1986), 365 pp., and *Tell of His Power* (Cherry Valley CA: The Cherrystone Press, 1988), 309 pp.
5. W. H. Branson, *Drama of the Ages* (Washington, D.C.: Review and Herald Publishing Association, 1953) 81, 101.
6. Cited in Zurcher, *op. cit.,* 146.
7. I am including this *Bible Readings* statement in full, because it later opened up this particular issue in the QOD debate. To my knowledge, I don't think anyone outside of the very few who were responsible for the revision even knew of the revised editing. It surely threw kerosene on the smoldering fire.
8. I am indebted to Ralph Larson for pointing out to me Anderson's amazing explanation of why the 1915 *Bible Readings for the Home Circle* had to be purged.
9. In the Annotated edition of QOD we are given a host of indications that the 1957 QOD was less than a fair, reliable treatment of Adventist thought, such as page xv, "less than transparent;" xxx, "push the facts a bit too far;" xxx, "present their data in a way that creates a false impression;" xxxiv, "misleading title;" 41, "masks the fact;" 45, "in a historic sense, false;" 324, "not accurate;" 516, "a misleading heading;" 517, "less than straightforward;" 52, "manipulation of the data;" 521 "had not told the truth;" 522 "elements of betrayal in the manipulation of data and in untruths;" 524, "misleading heading."

10. Ellen White, *Medical Ministry,* 181.

11. Ellen White, *Review and Herald,* August 22, 1907.

12. First Epistle to Cledonius, *Patrologia Graeca,* ed. J. P. Migne in Harry Johnson, *The Humanity of the Saviour* (London: The Epworth Press, 1962), 129.

13. Ellen White, *Patriarchs and Prophets,* 373.

14. Ellen White, *The Desire of Ages,* 49.

15. "When the fruit is brought forth, immediately he putteth in the sickle, because the harvest is come." Christ is waiting with longing desire for the manifestation of Himself in His church. When the character of Christ shall be perfectly reproduced in His people, then He will come to claim them as His own.

    "It is the privilege of every Christian not only to look for but to hasten the coming of our Lord Jesus Christ, (2 Peter 3:12, margin). Were all who profess His name bearing fruit to His glory, how quickly the whole world would be sown with the seed of the gospel. Quickly the last great harvest would be ripened, and Christ would come to gather the precious grain." White, *Christ Object Lessons,* 69.

16. White, T*he Youth's Instructor*, Oct. 20, 1886.

17. Ellen White, *Signs of the Times,* May 30, 1895.

18. For one response to the use of Ellen White's Letter 8, 1895 to Pastor W. L. H. Baker, see Ralph Larson's, *The Word Made Flesh,* 310-329.

19. J. R, /Zurcher, *Touched With Our Feelings* (Hagerstown, MD: Review and Herald Publishing Association, 1999), 146.

20. See Appendix B, "Ellen White's Use of Words Such as Passions, Inclinations, Propensities, Corruptions, etc."

21. Ellen White, Manuscript 303, 1903, cited in *Review and Herald,* February 17, 1994.

22. Henry Melvill, (1798-1871) Anglican preacher whose sermon, "The Humiliation of the Man Christ Jesus," was retitled, "Christ's Man's Example," and published in the *Review and Herald,* July 5, 1887. Melvill was an Anglican preacher who regularly filled his church of more than 2000 worshippers weekly.

23. Octavius Winslow, *The Glory of the Redeemer* (London: John Farquhar Shaw, 1853).

24. See earlier footnote regarding W.H.L. Baker and Ralph Larson's response to Ellen White's Letter.

25. White, *The Desire of Ages,* 117.

26. White, *Manuscript Releases,* Vol. 16, 181, 182.

27. White, *The Desire of Ages*, 512.

28. White, *Selected Messages,* Bk. One, 267, 268.

29. Melvill, *op. cit.*

30. Walter A. Elwell, *Evangelical Dictionary of Theology* (Grand Rapids, MI: Baker Book House, 1984), 413, 414.

31. See Herbert E. Douglass, *Messenger of the Lord* (Nampa, ID: Pacific Press Publishing Association, 1998), 378–380, 413.

32. See Harry Johnson, *The Humanity of the Savior* (London: The Epworth Press, 1962), 1–230.

33. Nam, *op. cit.*, 273.

34. 1957 QOD, 347.

35. Ibid., 341.

36. This insight and many more like it were the background of Andreasen's charge that the QOD trio had little understanding of the immense purpose of Christ's work as High Priest in His mediatorial work. That lack of grasping the larger view of what Christ was doing today in the Heavenly Sanctuary drove Andreasen unceasingly in his grievances concerning what Martin and the world were getting. He understood the implication of many Ellen White quotations that said, "In consequence of limited views of the sufferings of the divine Son of God, many place a low estimate upon the great work of atonement.. . . . The Father has given the world into the hands of Christ, that through his mediatorial work he may completely vindicate the binding claims and the holiness of every principle of his law." White, *Signs of the Times,* August 7, 1879.

37. For instance: "Those who cannot see the force of the sacred claims of God's law cannot have a clear and definite understanding of the atonement." *Signs of the Times,* August 14, 1879.

38. White, *The Great Controversy,* 420.

39. White, *The Desire of Ages,* 790.

40. Ibid., 671.

41. White, *The Great Controversy,* 422, 480.

♦ SIX ♦

Missing the Opportunity of the Century

Anyone reading what Andreasen was reading would also have felt nettled and disappointed by church leaders who were surely missing the opportunity of a century. But those who supposedly "read" the page proofs of QOD didn't bother to read the context of this "benefits of the atonement" statement nor many later congruent statements in the *Conflict* series. They too were also part of the missed opportunity of a century.

For many involved, however, including the General Conference president, the clumsy statements in QOD seemed to demolish Andreasen's concerns. But Andreasen and others knew that these carefully cherry-picked quotations portrayed a limited understanding of the Adventist doctrine of the atonement and could be easily accepted by the Evangelicals.

To repeat, QOD's selected quotations did not embrace the fuller understanding that Adventists had taught for many years. For instance, "And everyone who will break from the slavery and service of Satan, and will stand under the blood-stained banner of Prince Immanuel, will be kept by Christ's intercessions. Christ, as our Mediator, at the right hand of the Father, ever keeps us in view, for it is as necessary that He should keep us by His intercessions as that He should redeem us with His blood. If He lets go His hold of us for one moment, Satan stands ready to destroy. *Those purchased by His blood, He now keeps by His intercession.* He ever liveth to make intercession for us. 'Wherefore He is able also to save them to the

uttermost that come unto God by Him, seeing He ever liveth to make intercession for them' Heb. 7:25" (emphasis supplied).[1]

So much was left unsaid—and that was the pity and the essence of Andreasen's concern, as well as the concern of others. Andreasen knew Adventist thought far better than any of the QOD trio. His filing system was probably the most inclusive, private collection of Ellen White materials known anywhere. He knew that page 488 of *The Great Controversy* was as clear as the noonday sun: "Satan invents unnumbered schemes to occupy our minds, that they may not dwell upon the very work with which we ought to be best acquainted. The archdeceiver hates the great truths that bring to view an atoning sacrifice and an all-powerful mediator. He knows that with him everything depends on his diverting minds from Jesus and His truth.

"Those who would share the benefits of the Saviour's mediation should permit nothing to interfere with their duty to perfect holiness in the fear of God. The precious hours, instead of being given to pleasure, to display, or to gain seeking, should be devoted to an earnest, prayerful study of the word of truth. The subject of the sanctuary and the investigative judgment should be clearly understood by the people of God. All need a knowledge for themselves of the position and work of their great High Priest. Otherwise it will be impossible for them to exercise the faith which is essential at this time or to occupy the position which God designs them to fill."

Here is another typical example of Ellen White's understanding of the ellipse of truth—Atoning Sacrifice and All-powerful Mediator. We can't have one without the other, anymore than we can find water without hydrogen and oxygen!

Again, Why Was Andreasen Upset?

The question arises—about what was Andreasen upset in his attacks on the atonement issue? The best way to understand Andreasen's concern is to see the situation through his eyes. I will let Andreasen speak for himself as he reviewed Froom's editorials, beginning with Froom's February article in *Ministry,* to which we have already referred. (These were unpublished, private letters written to the president of the General Conference. Andreasen was a highly principled man who, throughout his ministry, was respectful of church leadership as his contemporaries well knew.)

Let's role-play with Andreasen:

February 15, 1957: Andreasen was astonished that Froom said that the QOD revision of the doctrine of the atonement was because "no one had taken the time for the sustained effort involved in laborious, comprehen-

sive search [in the writings of the Spirit of Prophecy] to find, analyze, and organize them." Previous church leaders were "largely unaware of this latent evidence and its priceless value: the need was not felt, and the time required for such a vast project was not considered available."

This was too much for Andreasen, in view of the many books that previous thought-leaders had written, in addition to his own excellent, synoptic studies on the sanctuary doctrine and the atonement.

Andreasen could see that Froom's narrow understanding of the atonement was missing the grand picture that Adventists have studied for most of a century—that Christ on the cross was not the beginning or the end of the suffering that sin brought to the heart of God.[2] In other words, the cost to God of the atonement is not to be measured by the hours on the cross. He saw Froom's problem—he had too limited views of the atonement.

Further, Andreasen wrote: "To rush into print at this time with shallow and confused ideas; to announce to the world that the theories set forth in the article under consideration is the Adventist understanding of the atonement, is unfortunate and is not true."[3]

October 15, 1957: The question now focused on Froom's statement that Christ's sacrificial act of the cross [is] complete, perfect, and final atonement for man's sin." Andreasen appealed to the denomination's "Declaration of the Fundamental Principles of the Seventh-day Adventists"[4] which said: "Jesus Christ . . . ascended on high to be our only Mediator in the Sanctuary in Heaven, where, with His own blood, He makes atonement for our sins: which atonement, so far from being made on the cross, which was but the offering of the sacrifice, is the very last portion of his work as priest, according to the example of the Levitical priesthood: which foreshadowed and prefigured the ministry of our Lord in heaven."[5]

If only the Adventist trio had sat down with Andreasen before publication, it seems obvious that careful rewording would have eliminated what seemed to be a grievous error.

November 4, 1957: Again, the issue revolved around what happened on the cross. If Calvinists are correct in insisting that Christ's death was the Day of Atonement, then Adventists for a century had been wrong. Andreasen quoted extensively from Uriah Smith, J. H. Waggoner, C. H Watson, plus many Ellen White references.

Further, Andreasen was astonished at Froom's question regarding Ellen White: "Why in our early days, did not Mrs. White point out and correct the limited or sometimes erroneous concepts of some of our early writers concerning the atonement? Why did she employ some of the restricted

phrases without contrasting, at the same time, her own larger, truer meaning when using them?" Then Froom answered his own question: "*No doctrinal truth of prophetic interpretation ever came to this people through the Spirit of Prophecy—not a single case*" (Froom's own emphasis).[6]

This kind of thinking requires more than a strong assertion. Andreasen turned to Ellen White's own words: "Often we remained together until late at night, and sometimes through the entire night, praying for light and studying the Word. Again and again these brethren came together to study the Bible, in order that they might know its meaning, and be prepared to teach it with power. When they came to the point in their study where they said, 'We can do nothing more,' the Spirit of the Lord would come upon me, I would be taken off in vision, and a clear explanation of the passages we had been studying would be given me, with instruction as to how we were to labor and teach effectively. Thus light was given that helped us to understand the scriptures in regard to Christ, His mission, and His priesthood. A line of truth extending from that time to the time when we shall enter the city of God, was made plain to me, and I gave to others the instruction that the Lord had given me.

"During this whole time I could not understand the reasoning of the brethren. My mind was locked, as it were, and I could not comprehend the meaning of the scriptures we were studying. This was one of the greatest sorrows of my life. I was in this condition of mind until all the principal points of our faith were made clear to our minds, in harmony with the Word of God. The brethren knew that when not in vision, I could not understand these matters, and they accepted as light direct from heaven the revelations given."[7]

The point Andreasen was making is that Froom was either ignorant of his Adventist history—or the QOD trio is, here and in other places, downgrading Ellen White.

November 14, 1957: Andreasen is still concerned (although he may have misunderstood Froom) with the wording that "the death of Christ [was] the complete sacrificial atonement for sin" (QOD 30). Again, he cites more Adventist scholars who had taught the larger view, and he lists them as evidence that "there is too much at stake to leave any doubt in the mind of the reader." No one could read these letters and not "see" or "feel" the anguish of the veteran Adventist scholar who sensed that the central feature of Adventist theology was being compromised.

He referred to copious quotations from *The Great Controversy* and for the first time submitted the clearest Ellen White statements of all that could be quoted. If only the Adventist trio had quoted and emphasized

these statements, it seems to me that Andreasen would have had no reason to continue his warnings: "The intercession of Christ in man's behalf in the sanctuary above is as essential to the plan of salvation as was His death upon the cross. By His death He began that work which after His resurrection He ascended to complete in heaven. We are now living in the great day of atonement." And then he added White's appeal: "Now, while our great High Priest is making the atonement for us, we should seek to become perfect in Christ."[8]

We can see that the 80-year-old veteran had the big picture of the plan of salvation in mind, which had no *limited* views of the atonement—he was in the major leagues, while the QOD trio remained in the minor leagues, playing a theological game with other minor league players, especially in discussing the atonement.

As Jerry Moon said so eloquently in 1988: "Much more might have been accomplished had the conferees [QOD trio] been able to show the evangelicals the significance of the investigative judgment as the logical extension and refinement of Arminianism and the blotting out of sins as essential to the completion of a universe-wide atonement."[9]

December 2, 1957: Andreasen reviewed Froom's editorials again with added insights regarding the historic Adventist understanding of the big picture of the Atonement. Probably no person alive in 1957 had a more extensive library of Ellen White writings; his index system was a marvel to those who saw it and this was before any attempts had been made by the White Estate to formally index her writings.

Those most familiar with Ellen White theology recognize her profound insight into the elliptic nature of biblical truth[10]—the symbiotic union of the objective and subjective aspects of all truth, such as grace-faith, Savior-Mediator, for-us in-us and through-us, justification-sanctification, forgiven-cleansed, law-gospel, etc. In other words, we can't have one without the other. In this way, Andreasen could easily appreciate Ellen White's wording that our Lord's High Priest ministry is just as important as His death on the cross. And any dimming of this symbiotic relationship became a red flag to his brilliant mind.

He was especially disturbed when he read Froom's defense: "When, therefore one hears an Adventist say, or reads in Adventist literature—even in the writings of Ellen G. White—that Christ is making atonement now, it should be understood that we mean simply that Christ is now *making application of the benefits of the sacrificial atonement He made on the cross;* that He is making it efficacious for us individually, according to our needs and requests."[11]

(When keen Adventists read that the QOD trio was telling the world that they now were the experts as to what Ellen White meant, using the words, "it should be understood," a great big exclamation point goes up! That was the underlying Achilles' heel of QOD. For Andreasen and others, this pervading hubris tainted even the best of their effort.)

January 5, 1958: Here, Andreasen reiterated his concerns of the past year and noted, regarding his observations in Froom's February 1957 article in *Ministry* that "there has been no renouncement of the doctrines, no public repudiation of the new ideas set forth, nor any public reprimand. We are, therefore, warranted in believing that the article under consideration speaks for the denomination." Amazing, to read this today!

Andreasen went further in analyzing the QOD trio's response to Martin's question on p. 341 of QOD: "Seventh-day Adventist have frequently been charged with teaching that the atonement was not completed on the cross. Is this charge true?" Andreasen opined that the trio could have answered in the words of Elder Nichol, as used in his *Review and Herald* 1952 July editorials that we referred to earlier. Andreasen then dissected the trio's answer, calling it "unique" and "evidently confused," especially when "bloodless atonements" are mentioned.

Before ending this letter he referred to two letters from the General Conference officers asking him to cease his activities and if not, it "will undoubtedly bring up the matter of your relationship to the church." In prescience, Andreasen said that "this is the approved and diplomatic way of saying that my credential and sustentation will be affected."[12]

January 19, 1958: Andreasen reviewed his former letters, each review using fresh logic and new information. He mentions the defection of A. F. Ballenger, a much-respected evangelist at the turn of the twentieth century. Andreasen noted that "the heresy for which he was dismissed is the very doctrine now being forced upon us, teaching that the atonement was made on the cross." In one way, Andreasen was correct but he was overlooking the QOD trios' intentions amidst their bumbling explanations. Thus, he overstated his objections.[13]

January 31, 1958: Andreasen continued his dissection of QOD's understanding of a "bloodless atonement"—that Christ's "blood" was efficacious only on the Cross and not involved in our Lord's work in the Holy and Most Holy Places in the heavenly sanctuary. He knew many Ellen White statements say otherwise. In other words, "the 'new view' entirely denies the blood atonement in the sanctuary" contrary to the Old and New Testament descriptions.[14] For instance, the death of the victim is not the atonement. It is after the goat was slain that the high priest

"goeth into make atonement in the holy place. Lev. 16:17." Andreasen emphasized that the atonement was made when the high priest went in to make atonement in the holy place, not outside in the court. See also Hebrews 9:7, 11, 12.

September 1960: Andreasen now looked back on the published QOD (1957) and on Martin's 1960 book *The Truth About Seventh-day Adventistm.* On page 15 of Martin's book is a statement signed by H. W. Lowe, chairman, Bible Study and Research Group of the General Conference of Seventh-day Adventists, that said in part: "His [Martin's] presentation of our doctrines and prophetic interpretations as found on pages 47–86 is accurate and comprehensive. . . . The reader will not overlook the fair and accurate statements of Adventist teachings so clearly set forth on pages mentioned above, 47–86." Again, "This author has earned our gratitude and respect for his earnest endeavor to set forth correctly our doctrinal positions and by his attitude of Christian brotherhood."[15]

In Martin's opinion, what hinders Adventist's full acceptance of the Evangelicals is our older Adventist literature which "is still in circulation," and which "teach some of the divergent views of Seventh-day Adventism . . . . It must be remembered that it will take time for divergent literature within the denomination to be brought under editorial control, and harmonized with the declared denominational position. The Adventists are seriously studying this problem."

For Andreasen, a long-time Adventist scholar especially skilled in the very subjects being discussed in both books (QOD and Martin's book), the trauma had to be most troubling. But then there was the Cleveland General Conference in 1958, which Martin referred to in his book: "The General Conference meeting in quadrennial session in Cleveland in 1958, thought the book [QOD] was sufficiently in harmony with Adventist views to preclude any necessity of even reviewing the issue. Its approach was apparent to all, as was its acceptance."[16] Martin had a point!

"Outright Deceit"

Finally, in his 1960 letter, Andreasen, after expressing his disappointment over QOD's treatment of the atonement, came to the "worst" of the distortions of Adventist doctrine—"it attacks the character of God, and accuses both the Father and the Son of outright deceit. Here is the QOD statement: 'Although born in the flesh, He was nevertheless God, and was exempt from the inherited passions and pollutions that corrupt the natural descendants of Adam.'"[17, 18]

Then Andreasen quoted p. 49 of *The Desire of Ages,* which we have

looked at earlier. His comment: "Christ was not *exempt* from the working of the great law of heredity. He accepted it."[19]

After a discussion of "temptations"—whether from God who tests or from Satan who tempts to make men and women to fall into evil habits—Andreasen quotes several Ellen White paragraphs:

> "These were real temptations, no pretense. . . . It was enough. Satan could go no further.
>
> . . . The severity of this conflict no human mind can compass. The welfare of the whole human family and of Christ Himself was at stake. . . . Human power was ready to fail. But all heaven sang the song of eternal victory. The human family have all the help that Christ had in their conflicts with Satan. They need not be overcome.
>
> . . .The Son of God in His humanity wrestled with the very same fierce, apparently overwhelming temptations that assail men—temptations to indulgence of appetite, to presumptuous venturing where God has not led them, and to the worship of the god of this world, to sacrifice an eternity of bliss for the fascinating pleasures of this life. Everyone will be tempted, but the Word declares that we shall not be tempted above our ability to bear. We may resist and defeat he wily foe."[20]
>
> "He [Christ] was not exempt from temptation. The inhabitants of Nazareth were proverbial for their wickedness. The low estimate in which they were generally held is shown by Nathanael's question, 'Can there any good thing come out of Nazareth?' John 1:46. Jesus was placed where His character would be tested. It was necessary for Him to be constantly on guard in order to preserve His purity. He was subject to all the conflicts which we have to meet, that He might be an example to us in childhood, youth, and manhood."[21]
>
> "Unless there is a possibility of yielding, temptation is no temptation. Temptation is resisted when man is powerfully influenced to do a wrong action; and, knowing that he can do it, resists, by faith, with a firm hold upon divine power. This was the ordeal through which Christ passed. He could not have been tempted in all points as man is tempted, had there been no possibility of his failing."[22]

In other words, if Christ was tempted in all points as man is tempted but yet "exempt" in some way that other humans are not, underneath the plan of salvation God was not playing fair—how could He ask men and women to overcome as Jesus overcame (Revelation 3:21)? Andreasen believed that God would be practicing "outright deceit," in requiring something impossible.

"The Highest Infamy"

In closing comments in his September 1960 letter, Andreasen wrote explicit arguments for retaining Ellen White's understanding of Christ's

humanity: "Had God favored His Son, Satan would have had an argument that even God could not meet. God sent His Son to show that He is not unjust in requiring obedience of Him. Christ came to earth to demonstrate God's justice. If God favored His Son, He would in that act have admitted that man cannot keep the law, that it was necessary for God to *exempt* Christ from some of the requirements He had imposed upon man. This would be for God to admit defeat. Moreover, it would have vitiated the whole plan of salvation. If Christ had received favors or exemptions, He would thereby have admitted Satan's claim that it is impossible for man to do God's will.

"Perish the thought that God in any way favored Christ! To teach or believe such is the highest of infamy, in that it is an indictment of God Himself, and accusing Him of deceit. It would be one of Satan's masterpieces to have His denominated people accept such doctrine.

"The matter we have been discussing here in regard to Christ being exempt from the passions and pollutions that corrupt the natural descendants of Adam, we consider one of the most heinous of the many departures from the faith which a study of the book *Questions on Doctrine* reveals.... That God miraculously *exempted* Him, as He did not exempt the rest of humanity; that He favored Christ so that He *could* not sin, was *heathenism of the worst kind*."[23]

Flash Points in later *Eternity* Editorials

During this time of *private* communication to Figuhr and, later, the QOD trio, Andreasen was reading and rereading Barnhouse and Martin's five editorials in *Eternity*, during 1956 and 1957. Much of what they had written was surprisingly cordial and accurate. But several points aroused Andreasen's fears.

To be historically faithful to reality in the late 50s, *we should role-play with Andreasen and think as he thought*. For instance:

In his September 1957 *Eternity* editorial, Barnhouse wrote. "They [the QOD trio] further explained to Mr. Martin that they had among their number certain members of their 'lunatic fringe' even as there are similar wild-eyes irresponsibles in every field of fundamental Christianity. . . . The position of the Adventists seems to some of us in certain cases to be a new position; to them it may be merely the position of the majority group of sane leadership which is determined to put the brakes on any members who seek to hold divergent from that of the responsible leadership of the denomination. . . . [The investigate judgment] to me, is the most colossal, psychological, face-saving phenomenon in religious

history! . . . Further, they do not believe, as some of their earlier teachers taught, that Jesus' atoning work was not completed on Calvary but instead that He was still carrying on a second ministering work since 1844. . . . [Regarding the investigative judgment since 1844] we personally do not believe that there is even a suspicion of a verse in Scripture to sustain such a peculiar position, and we further believe that any effort to establish it is *stale, flat, and unprofitable!*"

How would any of us have reacted to this editorial *written after QOD had been published,* if you had the theological insights of Andreasen, or most any other Adventist pastor, editor, or teacher?

In Martin's editorial in *Eternity* September 1957, he again characterized himself and Barnhouse as representatives of "historic orthodoxy" (meaning Calvinism and not including Arminians such as the Methodists, Nazarenes etc.) After recognizing that Adventists "have always as a majority, held to the cardinal, fundamental doctrines of the Christian faith which are necessary to salvation, and to the growth in grace that characterizes all true Christians believes, he then listed seven areas of disagreement. These were conditional immortality (including the annihilation of the wicked), sanctuary doctrine and the investigative judgment, the scapegoat (a teaching concerning Satan), the seventh-day Sabbath, Spirit of Prophecy, health reform, and the remnant church.

In Barnhouse's November 1957, *Eternity,* editorial, after noting the cordial interchanges of the previous two years, he referred again to how one Adventist writer "in particular set forth that Jesus Christ had a sinful human nature. The present volume [QOD] approaches this statement from several different points of view and repudiates it with horror. Because this has been made such a large issue by one 'defender of the faith,' who has attempted to pin this error on Mrs. White herself, the Adventist leaders in this present volume boldly present thirty-six different quotations from the writings of Mrs. White expressing herself in the strongest fashion in positive statements concerning the eternal Godhead and sinless human nature of our Lord. In another appendix are listed more than fifty quotations concerning the mystery of the incarnation in which Mrs. White expresses over and over the wonder of the Word made flesh and the glory of His sinlessness. The original difficulty arose from the fact that Mrs. White was not a trained theologian. She was unaware that some of her terms might be construed against her. In my opinion she lacked profundity, accuracy, and scholarship, but she owned, honored, and taught Jesus Christ as the eternal, sinless Son of God."

Suppose the Annotated Edition of QOD was read by Barnhouse and Martin

How would Barnhouse and Martin have felt if the Annotated Edition of QOD had been printed in their lifetime? How would they have responded to the Adventist trio if he discovered that QOD's misuse of Ellen White quotations should have made a trained theologian weep?

Adventist Professionals, Not Asleep

But laypersons around the United States were not asleep. An Adventist printer and first elder, Al Hudson, in Baker, Oregon, had lawyers who contracted with him to print their briefs for submission to the Oregon Supreme Court. Following their format, Hudson prepared a "Supporting Brief" for a proposed Resolution to be submitted to the delegates to the 1958 General Conference in Cleveland, Ohio. It read:

"Let it be resolved, that in view of the evidence presented, the book *Seventh-day Adventists Answer Questions on Doctrine* does not represent the faith and belief of the Seventh-day Adventist Church and is hereby repudiated on the following five points:

1) It contains specimens of scholastic and intellectual dishonesty.

2) It contains duplicity.

3) It is inadequate.

4) It contains error.

5) It is Satan's masterpiece of strategy to defeat the purpose of God for the Seventh-day Adventist Church.

In the balance of the Brief, much evidence was given to support the five charges. The Brief was ignored and never presented to the delegates. Hudson wrote to both Martin and Barnhouse and received no replies.

Telephone Conversation

However, on May 16, 1958, Hudson had a lengthy telephone conversation with Dr. Barnhouse. Some of Barnhouse's comments are as follows:

"All I'm saying is that the Adventists are Christians. I still think their doctrines are about the screwiest of any group of Christians in the world. I believe this beyond any question. In fact, the doctrine of the investigative judgment is the most blatant face-saving proposition that ever existed to cover up the debacle of the failure of Christ to come in 1844 as they said.

"The Adventists are wrong in keeping Saturday, the Protestants are

wrong in keeping Sunday, and that the only thing to keep is, to have the attitude that every day is alike and that God is not entering into this day, but He hates the Sabbath today. . . .

"[Regarding Ellen White] she was just a human being in the first place. Now I recognize clearly that Mrs. White very frequently wrote some very spiritual things, but God Almighty never spoke through a woman. Let's face it. You can't justify a woman preaching and usurping authority over a man. It can't be done. . . .

[Regarding Christ's human nature] Hudson asked Barnhouse: "They [Adventist trio] are taking the position, are they not, that Christ has the nature of Adam before he sinned, isn't that true?" Barnhouse replied: "I hope not! . . . Adam was a created being subject to fall. Jesus Christ was the God-man, not subject to fall." Hudson answered: "And that's your understanding of the position of our leaders?" Barnhouse: "Of course! They have taken it so strongly and it is their book [QOD]. . . . You see, if you do not believe that Jesus Christ is the eternal, sinless Son of God, that He could have not sinned, and . . . we have eighteen quotations from Mrs. White saying the same thing . . . and denying what you are telling me."

From this conversation, even this mere sampling, you can see how easy it is for Christian leaders to completely misunderstand each other, even when they use the same words! *We cannot use the weasel excuse that it is all a matter of semantics!* That would reveal outright ignorance of what is going on.

Chief Issue: Connection Between Christology and Eschatology

As all theologians can be measured by their linkage between their Christology and their eschatology, Andreasen was as clear as the noonday sun. However, the QOD trio, departed from a century of Adventist thinking. In their attempt to please the Evangelicals, they wandered away from copious biblical texts and forgot to read Ellen White's *The Great Controversy*, chapter by chapter, for example. *Andreasen's careful connection between Christology and Eschatology was the chief issue separating him from the General Conference President and the QOD trio.* Andreasen got his theological vector from statements such the following:

> "Now, while our great High Priest is making the *atonement* for us, we should seek to become perfect in Christ. Not even by a thought could our Saviour be brought to yield to the power of temptation. Satan finds in human hearts some point where he can gain a foothold; some sinful desire is cherished, by means of which his temptations assert their power. But Christ declared of Himself: 'The prince of this world cometh, and hath nothing in Me.' John 14:30. Satan could find nothing in the Son of

God that would enable him to gain the victory. He had kept His Father's commandments, and there was no sin in Him that Satan could use to his advantage. This is the condition in which those must be found who shall stand in the time of trouble."[24]

Reality Check

Andreasen thought it unfortunate to focus on topics such as "perfection" and "the nature of Christ" without equal or even greater focus on Christ Himself, who will be the agent of perfecting human character through His Holy Spirit.[25] "The truth as it is in Jesus," a common Ellen White phrase, simply means that: the more we focus on Jesus as our closest and best Friend, the more we let His words become our daily nourishment, the more "natural" and "habitual" we will be relentlessly pursuing moral perfection.[26] Moral perfection is an attitude more than it is an attainment; even after 100,000 years into eternity, we will still be pursuing "perfection." But this attitude must be based on accepting truthful principles of who Jesus really is and why He came the way He did[27] and why He died.[28] Or else we will still be in Babylon and not know it!

Hancock's Research in 1962

Coming like the glow of Indian Summer after some killer frosts, Robert Lee Hancock's 1962 thesis entitled "The Humanity of Christ," at the Seventh-day Adventist Theological Seminary is perhaps the last to be written at the seminary on this subject from his and Andreasen's point of view. In his three-part conclusion, Hancock wrote:

"Regarding the specific question of Christ's humanity, this study has revealed that:

1) From its earliest days the Seventh-day Adventist Church has taught that when God partook of humanity He took, not the perfect, sinless nature of man before the Fall, but the fallen, sinful, offending, weakened, degenerate nature of man as it existed when He came to earth to help man. . . .

2) That during the fifteen-year period between 1940 and 1955 the words 'sinful' and 'fallen' with reference to Christ's human nature were largely or completely eliminated from denominational published materials. . . .

3) That since 1952, phrases such as 'sinless human nature,' 'nature of Adam before the fall,' and 'human nature undefiled,' have taken the place of the former terminology. . . . The findings of this study warrant the conclusion that Seventh-day Adventist teachings regarding the human nature of Christ *have* changed and that these changes involve concepts and not merely semantics."[29]

Notes:

1. White, *Manuscript Releases,* vol. 15, 104 (emphasis supplied). Also, *Seventh-day Adventist Bible Commentary,* vol. 6, 1028.
2. Revelation 13:8, "the Lamb slain from the foundation of the world."
3. The M. L. Andreasen File," (St. Maries, ID: LMN Publishing International, 1993), 1–5.
4. Because of many accusations that Adventists believed "subversive" doctrines, one of which was that Adventists taught that the atonement was not made on the cross (which without further explanation is fatal to the whole sanctuary doctrine and the historical relevancy of the Adventist movement), James White felt impelled to issue this "creed" in the first issue of *Signs of the Times,* June 4, 1874.
5. Andreasen File, 11.
6. Ibid., 15–22.
7. White, *Selected Messages,* vol. 1, 207.
8. Andreasen File, 23–29.
9. Research paper, "M.L. Andreasen, L. E. Froom, and the Controversy over *Questions on Doctrine.*
10. See Appendix C: "The Elliptical Nature of Truth."
11. Andreasen File, 34–41.
12. Andreasen File, 66.
13. Ibid., 67–73.
14. Ibid., 77.
15. F. D. Nichol wrote to R. R. Figuhr, March 10, 1960 that "the non-Adventist world would take Lowe's words as a kind of endorsement of the book." Further, "I don't think we should ever have put such a prefatory page in a book that is subtly attempting to show that many of our teachings are wrong." Cited in Nam, *op. cit., 394.*
16. Ibid., 393.
17. Ibid., 383.
18. Ibid.
19. Andreasen File, 91.
20. White, *Selected Messages,* bk. 1, 95.
21. White. *The Desire of Age,* 71.
22. White, *The Youth's Instructor,* July 20, 1899.
23. Andreasen File, 94.
24. White, *The Great Controversy,* 623 (emphasis supplied).
25. Among his several books, Andreasen's *The Faith of Jesus* was perhaps his most systematic presentation of Adventist theology:"Let us study the faith of Jesus, not as a matter of theology, but as a way of life," 12.

26. White, *Christ's Object Lessons,* 330. Lexus car motto: "The relentless pursuit of perfection."

27. See Appendix D: "Why Jesus Came the Way He Did."

28. See Appendix E: "Why Jesus Died."

29. Hancock may not have been aware of.1) F. D. Nichol's editorials in July, 1952, (mentioned earlier) in which he dealt specifically with this subject and 2) W. H. Branson's *Drama of the Ages,* to which we referred earlier. Other than these two items, Hancock was clear as a foghorn in San Francisco Bay.

♦ SEVEN ♦

Fifty Years of Muddle

One of the many movements within Adventism that grew out of the perceived errors that were leading up to and including QOD is formally called *The 1888 Message Study Committee.* Among its leaders have been Donald Short and Robert Wieland. The embedded connection between this 1888 Message group and QOD should be further examined, as well as the several unfortunate reconstructions/revisions of what really went on in the 1888 Minneapolis General Conference.

The last fifty years of muddle centered on two attempts to rewrite Adventist history. One attempt focused on the key doctrinal issues of why Jesus came the way He did and the significance of his High Priestly ministry. The other rewrite has been the concurrent reluctance to review the theological detour that occurred, when denominational publications and academic classrooms opined that the key contribution of the 1888 General Conference was to recognize that Adventists had finally recovered the so-called emphasis of the Protestant Reformers regarding "righteousness by faith." Nothing was farther from the truth! This line of reasoning, wherever taught or preached, poisons any genuine study of that remarkable conference. Further, it has locked the door on what Ellen White called "a most precious message"—a message that would prepare a people for translation. Some day, that door will be unlocked.

Many other groups, often called "independent ministries," have flowed

through the Adventist community on all continents in response to what they have seen as the flaws of QOD. Each of them would not have seen the light of day had QOD not been published.

Quick Overview of Adventist Disarray Since the 1960s

The theological contours affected by QOD were far more serious than what appeared on the surface, especially the humanity of Christ and sanctuary issues. Many teachers, pastors, and laypeople continued to see the issues clearly—that one cannot separate or reframe Christology without immediately affecting one's eschatology. Andreasen saw it early on. In support of QOD, church leaders, in workers' meetings and in various publications, soon began treating as equally heretical emphases: 1) Christ's post-fall nature and 2) overcoming sin this side of the Second Advent.

An amazing spirit of retaliation against those who differed with QOD soon was endemic. Heavily advertised publications appeared, focusing on "perfection" (overcoming sin) as an impossibility while still in "sinful flesh." In so doing, a novel definition of "perfection" was created, at least for Adventists, in the place of the time-honored understanding of human cooperation with divine power in overcoming sin, here and now.[1]

All this was given impetus when the QOD trio bought into classic Calvinism regarding the humanity of Jesus. Thus, as surely as tomorrow's sunrise, classic Adventist thought regarding eschatology was dramatically distorted—unless one is comfortable with non-sequiturs. Anyone not alive or still in elementary school in 1957 may find all this unbelievable!

Bull and Lockhart's Analysis of the Post-1960 Era, Especially at the Seminary

All this is not my opinion only. This shift in denominational thought, especially in our theological seminary, was clearly seen in Malcolm Bull and Keith Lockhart's second edition of their *Seeking a Sanctuary.* Probably no authors have focused more plainly on the influence of QOD and on how it dramatically affected the instruction of key seminary teachers for a generation, on such subjects as "righteousness-by faith," "the humanity of Christ," and the linkage between Christology and eschatology.

These two men saw immediately the impasse that arises when one is confused about the nature of sin—a confusion that Andreasen and Ellen White avoided. Bull and Lockhart recognized Australian layman Robert

Brinsmead's quandary, who assumed that there was "an unbridgeable gulf between human sinfulness and the need for perfection." Brinsmead's solution was to "emphasize the miraculous infusion of perfection through the cleansing of the heavenly sanctuary," because QOD had made perfection seem a remote possibility."[2] Brinsmead soon developed a worldwide following as a rebuke to the publication of QOD.

Edward Heppenstall, Chair of Systematic Theology[3]

In contrast to Brinsmead (as well as to Andreasen), Bull and Lockhart continued: "The focus on the crucifixion encouraged by *Questions on Doctrine* was taken further by the Adventist theologian, Edward Heppenstall. His solution to the difficulty of explaining how the sinner could reach perfection was to argue that perfection was neither necessary nor possible. In 1963 he stated that 'absolute perfection and sinlessness cannot be realized here and now.'"[4]

What was the theological paradigm into which Heppenstall had bought? Bull and Lockhart claimed: "This response, which in Adventist terms was far more radical than that of Brinsmead, was partly the product of Heppenstall's understanding of original sin, a concept that had not been much in evidence in Adventism until this time."[5]

How did this new understanding of sin affect Heppenstall's rejection of Andreasen's and the rest of Adventist thought before 1955, especially regarding the issue of the humanity of Christ?[6] Bull and Lockhart continued: "Heppenstall opposed the notion of Christ's fallen nature, because in his view, 'the efficacy of Christ's sacrifice lay in his absolute sinlessness.'"[7]

Thus for Heppenstall, his understanding of sin directly affected his understanding of both Christ's humanity and the traditional understanding of Adventism in regard to "overcoming sin." Note Bull and Lockhart's observation: "Prior to Heppenstall, no important Adventist writer denied the possibility of perfection."[8]

The issue also involves using different definitions for "perfection," "absolute perfection," "overcoming sin," etc.[9] But unspoken perspective and presuppositions affect the way anyone uses these phrases. For all of us, it depends on how we understand the sin problem and how Adam's posterity also becomes sinners.[10]

Change of Emphasis on Nearness of the Advent

But Bull and Lockhart saw how core theological thoughts don't stand alone—everything is connected to everything else. Our authors chronologically noted the amazing change of emphasis in Adventist teaching and

preaching after 1960. Using a late-1960 survey that indicated that "the Second Advent received less emphasis in the preaching of the church than thirty years previously," they asserted that "Heppenstall's emphasis on justification in the 1960s" was a "reaction to the new soteriology of *Questions on Doctrine*, the theory [that] the theology of justification can be viewed as a way of compensating for a decline in belief in an imminent Second Coming."[11]

Our authors continued: "Justification enables believers to be made righteous immediately rather than at the end of the world. . . . The wide appeal of justification in the 1960s indicated that by this point many Adventists were simply looking for an answer to the question of how perfection might be achieved in the present, rather than in an increasingly remote final generation of the future."[12]

Bull and Lockhart found evidence that "Heppenstall rarely mentioned the prospect of translation and never discussed the character of the last generation. Heppenstall broke the connection between Adventist soteriology and Adventist eschatology."[13]

As we turn back to QOD and Andreasen, we see more clearly how the two immensely important paradigms (Andreasen's and Heppenstall's) differed and vastly affected the future of the Adventist Church for a whole generation.

Unity and Coherence of Andreasen's Theological Paradigm

If Andreasen is correct in (1) his understanding of why Jesus came the way He did, and (2) if he is correct in his synoptic picture of why Jesus died and (3) why His incarnational ministry is completed in His High Priestly duties, and (4) if he is correct in his understanding of the Great Controversy issues—then His "last generation" scenario follows as day follows night. If one of our Lord's reasons to live and die as He did—demonstrating that men and women "in sinful flesh," as He had, could, in cooperation with the Holy Spirit, overcome sin completely—then the biblical pictures of a last generation being sealed with God's approval for their victory over sin in the worst of times follows logically. But also, many are the White references that reflect this connection between a correct understanding of our Lord's humanity and loyal believers who become overcomers in earth's last generation

White and Andreasen simply unfolded such biblical passages as 2 Peter 3, Revelation 7:1–4, and 14:6–16, among many.

For Andreasen, this straight line from the humanity of Christ through

the atonement in all of its phases fulfilled the gospel plan and met the purpose of the Great Controversy theme—changing rebels into loyal sons and daughters who rely on the Holy Spirit's empowerment. He also saw clearly how the century-old Adventist understanding of Christology and eschatology focuses on how Jesus and His loyalists proved Satan wrong and God fair and just. Changing one's understanding of the humanity of Christ immediately changes one's understanding of the several phases of the atonement and thus what may be expected in a last-generation scenario.[14]

Theological Liberalism

All the reactions to QOD must also include the rise of theological liberalism (some prefer the label, progressive) in the Adventist Church. Such church members responded to what was perceived as latent legalism in the church, especially on the emphasis that God expects His people to be overcomers "even as I [Jesus] overcame" (Revelation 2:21).

Instead of both groups (classicists and liberals) looking more thoughtfully at the Laodicean message of Revelation 3, both groups tended to build a deeper divide. Liberalism took courage in (1) QOD's confusion over Christology and its less-than-lucid explanation of Christ's high priestly ministry and (2) was especially comforted with the prevailing shift of Adventist thought regarding "overcoming sin"— and (3) took new courage in "new" thoughts explaining away the delay of the Advent.

Those who tended toward legalism (as some have been described) often focused on correct theology but not on the personal characteristics of Jesus that would make them more gracious in contending with the so-called liberal-progressive factions. Both groups tended to lose the big picture of the Great Controversy and its personal issues for each of us today.

QOD Magisterium

Many authors and teachers through the years swallowed some of the unsupportable conclusions of QOD (such as those Dr. Knight has pointed out in his Annotation), thus making QOD's assertions the accepted magisterium. In many ways the word has been out since the 1960s that pastors and teachers should not speak out on subjects such as the sanctuary and the humanity of Christ because such topics are *divisive. But when did the divisiveness begin?*

Perhaps what has been really unfortunate in the past fifty years has been the astounding attempt to ridicule M. L. Andreasen. For instance, in a recent book, Andreasen "is a good example of the improper use of her [Ellen

White's] writings." He "shows no evidence that he correctly understood inspiration from the Bible or Ellen White's writings." Or, that his "line of reasoning had many weaknesses, for example: It held an inadequate and non-biblical view of the nature of sin." Or that "many of the ideas of Andreasen were later taken to their logical conclusion by . . . Brinsmead, who caused havoc and division in the church during the 1960s."[15]

Then, in revealing his personal theological bias, the author correctly noted the main tenets of Andreasen's "final generation theology" but then dismissed them as non-biblical and a misuse of Ellen White's thought. Yet, he provided no proof that his assertions or conclusions were correct and that Andreasen was wrong.[16]

Alas, several other books have been unfortunately written in a similar vein.

Opportunity of the Century—What If?

What if the Adventist trio had not muted our understanding of the second angel's message of Revelation 14?

Adventist self-understanding involves its primary historical reason for existence—to call God's people out of Babylon, out of churches that have fallen for Satan's heresies, and to prepare them to live forever. Through the last 160 years or so, many laypersons have understood this emphasis in Revelation 14; they gladly and gratefully left their established churches and became happy, loyal Adventists. But then to watch their Adventist leaders go mute on this basic reason for the Adventist Church's existence—all this became a great concern for many in the past fifty years.

Though not a popular message, the Adventist message on Revelation 14 is a prophetic message of present truth. But Martin and Barnhouse, it seems, never were given even a clue as to the biblical basis for our allegiance to the three angels of Revelation 14.

What if Martin and Barnhouse were convinced that we had not repudiated our century-old conviction that God has challenged the world in the second angel's message?

What if Martin and Barnhouse were given the big picture of what is going on in the Great Controversy and how we are living in its closing days? Such was the opportunity of the century that was strangely ignored.

I cannot improve upon George Knight's evaluation that *Questions on Doctrines* easily qualifies as the most divisive book in Seventh-day Adventist history."[17]

Nor would I want to improve on John Milton: "Though all the winds of doctrine were let loose to play upon the earth, so Truth be in the field, we do ingloriously, by licensing and prohibiting, to misdoubt her strength. Let her and Falsehood grapple: who ever knew Truth put to the worse in a free and open encounter?"[18]

Or Socrates' advice to Charmides: "But what matter," said Charmides, "from whom I heard this?" "No matter at all," I [Socrates] replied: "for the point is not who said the words, but whether they are true or not."[19]

Notes:

1. A tsunami of new emphasis on what is meant by "perfection" emerged in the early 1960s. This subject became the litmus test for Adventist workers and laymen. This fallout from QOD generated dozens of "straw men," such as "living without a Mediator," "sin is built into human nature (birth-nature) and not merely a choice," "behavior is legalism," "perfect people think they can meet Satan on their own," "focusing on personal perfection overrides a focus on Jesus," etc.
2. Malcolm Bull and Keith Lockhart, *Seeking a Sanctuary*, Second Edition (Bloomington, IN: Indiana University Press, 2007), 86.
3. Ted Heppenstall and I had a remarkable relationship and, as with Froom, we never let our theological differences trouble our friendship. Whenever we attended various meetings, we would spend many evenings in our motel rooms talking over the business of the church. Only occasionally did we discuss the humanity of Christ or the difference between "moral perfection" and "absolute perfection."
4. "Is Perfection Possible? *Signs of the Times,* December 1963.
5. Malcolm Bull and Keith Lockhart, *op. cit.*, 87.
6. Heppenstall's long tenure at the Adventist Theological Seminary has been called the "Heppenstall hegemony."
7. Bull and Lockhart, *op. cit.,* 87. We today can better appreciate Heppenstall's commendation of the writers of *Question on Doctrine* in view of his merging theological leadership in the Adventist seminary: He said that the QOD trio had done "an excellent job" and declared the manuscript to be "the best that has been so far" in stating Adventist belief to the world." Cited in Nam, *op.cit.,* 248.
8. Ibid.
9. See *Perfection—The Impossible Possibility* (Nashville, TN: Southern Publishing Association, 1975), Four essays on "perfection," by Herbert E. Douglass, Edward Heppenstall, Hans K. LaRondelle, and C. Mervyn Maxwell.
10. See Appendix F: "What Do We Mean by Moral Perfection?"
11. Bull and Lockhart, *op. cit.,* 93. See also Graeme Bradford, *More Than a Prophet* (Berrien Springs, MI: Biblical Perspectives, 2006), 193: "The church [Seventh-day Adventist Church] had changed from its ideas on the nature of Christ, sinless perfectionism and the atonement due largely to the teachings of Heppenstall."
12. Ibid., 93, 94.

13. Ibid., 94.

14. For example: "When he comes he is not to cleanse us of our sins. He is not then to remove from us the defects in our characters. He will not then cure us of the infirmities of our tempers and dispositions. He will not do this work then. Before that time this work will all be accomplished, if wrought for us at all. Then those who are holy will be holy still. They are not to be made holy when the Lord comes. Those who have preserved their bodies, and their spirits, in holiness, and in sanctification, and honor, will then receive the finishing touch of immortality. And when he comes, those who are unjust, and unsanctified, and filthy, will remain so forever. There is then no work to be done for them which shall remove their defects, and give them holy characters. The Refiner does not then sit to pursue his refining process, and remove their sins, and their corruption. This is all to be done in these hours of probation. It is now that this work is to be accomplished for us. . . .

    "As we lay hold upon the truth of God, its influence must affect us. It must elevate us. It must remove from us every imperfection. It must remove from us sins of whatever nature. And it must fit us, that we may be prepared to see the king in his beauty, and finally to unite with the pure and heavenly angels in the kingdom of glory. This work is to be accomplished for us here. Here we are, with these bodies and spirits, which are to be fitted for immortality." ST, September 18, 1879 (First presented in Battle Creek, March 6, 1869, White, *Testimonies,* vol. 2, 355, 356).

15. Graeme Bradford, *op. cit.,* 188.

16. See Appendix G—What Do We Mean by "Final Generation"?

17. QOD, Annotated Edition, xiii.

18. John Milton, "Areopogitica." (1644), *The Harvard Classics,* ed., Charles W. Eliot (New York: P. F. Collier & Son Company, 1909, vol. 3), 239.

19. *The Dialogues of Plato,* Jewett, vol. 1, 11 (161).

♦ EIGHT ♦

The Unique Adventist Understanding of the Great Controversy

The issue in 1957 was the fatal attempt to meld (1) the limited understanding of the Adventist trio's understanding of what made Adventism work with (2) Augustinian/Calvinism's Sovereignty of God theme. *What could have made all the difference would have been a biblical review of the Great Controversy Theme in contrast to Calvinism's limited understanding of the character of God and the gospel.* The central question for both parties is: What does God plan to accomplish with His Salvation Plan?

Major Issues in the Great Controversy Theme[1]

In a few words, on God's side, the purpose of the Great Controversy Theme is to prove Satan wrong in his charges against God's character and His government.[2] The issue is always planted in God's created soil of Freedom. Before love, there had to be freedom. All created intelligences, beginning with the angels and extending throughout the inhabited worlds, were endowed with freedom—the freedom even to say No to God's plan for them. In other words, responsibility (ability-to-respond) was the actionable word—freedom to respond to their Creator, either positively or negatively. Love is an attribute found only in the larger embracing air of freedom. Throughout the biblical story, God was trying to make clear what He planned to accomplish with His salvation plan, as He manifested His fairness, love, and trustworthiness through His dealing with, first, the Israelites and eventually, in the person of Jesus Christ.

On the human side, the purpose of the Great Controversy Theme is to restore in willing men and women the image of Christ, their Maker. To do so, the Holy Spirit's task is to work out of a person's life all that sin has worked in. By God's grace, men and women, regardless of nationality and level of schooling, can be forgiven and transformed into overcomers who hate sin. People whom God and the angels can trust with eternal life will inhabit the redeemed world. No rebels will be granted eternal life. The highest motivation for God's loyalist is to honor God, not to merely impress Him.

Therefore, the following principles do follow:

1. The believer's character determines destiny, not merely one's profession of faith.

2. Perfection is a matter of continual moral growth and not a concern for arbitrary goalposts.

3. Christian growth rests on the profound linkage of human will and divine grace—the grace of pardon and the grace of power.

How does this all work out in theological talk?

Soteriology is the study of the plan of salvation. The life and work of Jesus should be one's chief consideration. How one thinks about Jesus directly affects all other biblical studies, especially eschatology, the study of last-day events.

For Calvinists, their Five Points' yardstick controls all aspects of their soteriology. Their understanding of the utter depravity of mankind rests on their notion of original sin and, thus, the companion doctrine that all men and women are born sinners. Their only explanation for the sinfulness of mankind was simply to declare that we all are sinners because Adam sinned. Because of their controlling "sovereignty of God" principle, mankind could not possibly have free will and thus any responsibility. If anyone were to be "saved," it would have to be due to God's sovereign choice, not man's response.

Therefore, for the Calvinist, if Jesus is man's Savior, He would have to die for those who are already elected to be saved. Further, our Lord could not have inherited, as we do, the genetic stream of His ancestors, because, if so, He too would have been born a sinner. The Calvinistic solution: Jesus had to be "exempt" from all inherited tendencies to sin—just as Roman Catholics had concluded. Thus, to make their major premise work, the elect would be those who were "given" faith and thus the "ability" to profess gratefulness for Christ's substitutionary atonement. Because they had been foreordained to be saved, the elect could not fall out of grace; they could never be "unsaved."

Adventist Template and Calvinist Template Incompatible

Obviously, Seventh-day Adventists should have great difficulty trying to harmonize their understanding of salvation with their Calvinist friends, no matter how much linguistic gymnastics they could muster. The problem in 1955–1957 was that foggy thinking on the part of the Adventists led them, almost unknowingly, into capitulating to the Evangelicals. Here began fifty years of focus on some kind of objective atonement without equal weight on the subjective aspect of the atonement that would have highlighted our Lord's work as our High Priest.

The Adventist trio were untrained theologians. They had not seen that 1) the Scriptures embrace a complete system of truth and that every part in the Bible should sustain and not contradict any other part; 2) that any defective or imperfect concept of any one doctrine must inevitably lead to confusion and error throughout the whole system, and 3) that two or more self-consistent systems of theology are possible, but they cannot both be biblically correct. For instance, it is impossible to join the tectonic plates of Augustianisn-Calvinism with either Pelagianism/SemiPelagianism or Arminian-Adventism. Unless, that is, one is prepared for a plethora of troubles.

This explains the volcanic eruptions that soon developed.

Obviously, Andreasen and Others Aroused

All this incompatibility aroused Andreasen and many others. The veteran theologian knew from personal study and experience that only those who acknowledge the binding claim of the moral law can explain the nature and purpose of the atonement—that when Jesus paid the indebtedness of the repentant sinner, He did not give him or her license to continue sinning but to now live responsibly in obedience to the law. Calvinists are not able to process this fundamental thought.

Because Andreasen started with the systematic principle of God's freedom and man's responsibility and not God's sovereignty and man's predestination, the veteran theologian saw immediately that the Adventist tectonic plate should be an unmovable theological mass.

Thus, the ruling principle of human responsibility led Andreasen toward a different understanding of the Atonement. He saw that the sanctuary doctrine (including the purpose of the Old Testament sanctuary service and its New Testament application as best described in the Book of Hebrews) painted a picture of the unbroken union between the objective and subjective aspects of the Atonement. From the moment Christ

was "slain from the foundation of the world" (Revelation 13:8) to the end of the millennium, when Satan and the consequences of sin will be no more, Andreasen could see what the Calvinists could not.

Biblical Sanctuary Doctrine[3]

The sanctuary doctrine emphasizes how God forgives and justifies only penitent men or women, but more! The doctrine equally emphasizes that God promises to empower the penitent so that sins are eliminated by the inner graces of the Holy Spirit. The penitent men and women who continue to cooperate with God will truly find the peace, assurance, and divine empowerment that comes in completing the gospel plan in their lives. This was never made clear to our Calvinist friends in 1957, and it has been one of the causes of Adventist theological muddle in the years since.[4]

Notes:

1. See Appendix A: "Issues in the Great Controversy."
2. "Great and marvelous are Your works, Lord God Almighty! Just and true are Your ways, O King of the saints" (Revelation 15:3). "For true and righteous are His judgments" (Revelation 19:2). For a biblical essay on how the Great Controversy Theme pervades the Scriptures, see the author's "God on trial," in *Ministry,* May 1982. For an extended unfolding of the Great Controversy Theme, see author's *God At Risk* (Roseville, CA: Amazing Facts, 2004), 408 pp.
3. Exegetical methodology, biblical theology, etc., have their limitations for each text, chapter, book, because their drilling for meaning depends on their presuppositions. Each scholar works with his own presupposition as he/she sifts biblical materials. "Only systematic theology provides the tools and disciplinary space for such a task . . . . Biblical theology requires a center from which to gather the vast variety of issues, histories, and teachings present in biblical texts. . . .Thus, the proper expression of the Sanctuary doctrine as hermeneutical vision of a complete and harmonious system of truth requires the contributions of new approaches to biblical and systematic theologies. . . . From this foundational level, the Sanctuary doctrine becomes the hermeneutical light guiding in the interpretation of these far-reaching ideas (hermeneutical conditions of theological method) and in the understanding of the complete and harmonious system of Christian theology." Fernando Canale, "From Vision to System," *Journal of the Adventist Theological Society,* 16/1, 2 (2005)
4. Canale is correct in his understanding of the necessity of a central hermeneutical principle for any theological system; for Adventist theology, Canale believes that foundation principle is the sanctuary doctrine. This is precisely what the QOD trio never seemed to understand. Note the following: "The scripture which above all others had been both the foundation and the central pillar of the advent faith, was the declaration, "Unto two thousand and three hundred days; then shall the sanctuary be cleansed (Daniel 8:14)."—White, *The Great Controversy*, 409. "The subject of the sanctuary was the key with unlocked the mystery of the disappointment of 1844. It

opened to view a complete system of truth, connected and harmonious," Ibid., 423. "Those who received the light concerning the sanctuary and the immutability of the law of God, were filled with joy and wonder, as they saw the beauty and harmony of the system of truth that opened to their understanding." Ibid., 454.

♦ NINE ♦

Fifty Years Later—What Should We Do to Rectify Mistakes?

Our first responsibility is to remember that what happened in 1957 was a wholesale detour from what Adventist theology was for a century. Some will say that was healthy and most needed. Obviously, if that were so, we would have seen through the last fifty year a fresh way of explaining the distinctiveness of Adventist theology. Unfortunately, the last fifty years have been the most divisive period throughout the Adventist world.

Let us role play and remember:

1. *Remember* that the Adventist trio and their confreres were not trained theologians. They were wholeheartedly indefatigable in their labors. Few, before or since, have invested more time and energy in denominational interests. I knew them personally; we became very close as their westering sun set. But, they were unaware of how modern theological entities are different, not because of semantic issues, but because their theological family tree is built on thinkers who had different and conflicting ideas of what God is like and how that affected their doctrines of salvation, etc.

   Ever since Hesiod around 700 B.C. began thinking about God,

theologians have begun their systematic thinking with their presuppositions, whether it be the prevailing philosophy or a particular assumption of what God is like. Either presupposition would then determine their theological methods as they spelled out the relationship between God and human beings on the basis of their paradigm. No theological system emerges without a presupposition or theory, none!.

2. *Remember* even more in our day that every theological system, whether Adventist, Calvinist, Lutheran, Anabaptist, Methodist, Roman Catholic, Orthodox Catholic, Buddhist, or Hindu, for examples, is based on the presuppositions of their favorite theologian or group of theologians. Obviously, all groups believe that their presuppositions are valid according to some standard, whether it be the Bible or the prevailing philosophical system such as Existentialism, Platonic Objectivism, or Subjective Rationalism, etc. If it be the Bible, then still the presupposition must be examined before its theological system should be given validity.

3. *Remember* that in 1957, the century-old, Adventist theological system was on firm ground when it bumped up against the Calvinistic plate—and the usual tectonic-plate earthquake was sensed throughout both worlds. Neither groups sensed the impossibility of "joining" both plates on central issues. They both thought that smoothing our rhetoric would produce a "meeting of minds."

4. *Remember* that the Adventist theological system is based on the Great Controversy Theme (GCT), a prevailing theme that is based on the whole Bible, from Genesis to Revelation, and not on any one book of the Bible. It is further illuminated by the writings of Ellen G. White that highlight this Biblical thread. The GCT accepts the biblical picture of God as the Loving, Merciful Creator who has made mankind able to respond to His love, a God who allowed evil to develop so that its malevolent practices could be recognized for all its awfulness. The GCT reveals a God whose Plan of Salvation aims at rescuing all the willing obedient from this evil planet and then entrusting them with eternal life.

   As I noted earlier, Fernando Canale has written clearly that the sanctuary doctrine is the clearest way to unfold the vast overview, coherency, and unity of the GCT. This has always been the open secret of classic Adventist thought.

5. *Remember* that thought leaders, including F. D. Nichol, W. H. Branson, Raymond Cottrell, Don Neufeld, M. L. Andreasen,

Kenneth H. Wood, of the 1950 years, had built their Adventist thinking on the basic interlocking logic of the GCT. To dismiss such leaders is hardly possible unless their emphasis and conclusions have been shown to be invalid and contrary to a "new" and better way of doing Adventist theology since 1957

6. *Remember* that a Christian theology can always be judged by its eschatology—that is, by its view of last-day events and the future of this planet. And one's eschatology is generally affected by one's Christology. Although this sounds over simplified, that's the way it turns out. How one thinks about the humanity of Christ most often affects one's view of what God expects out of His people in the last days.

7. *Remember* above all else, that the prophetic assignment of the Seventh-day Adventist Church as outlined in Revelation 7, 13, and 14, will be fulfilled by some generation of Adventists who recovers its distinctive message as outlined in the GCT.

Appendices

Appendix A: Issues in the Great Controversy Theme[1]

The great controversy that the Bible describes is far different than Hollywood's portrayal of a galactic clash of heavenly warriors with their shining swords. The great controversy is over the question of who can best govern the universe—and who presents the best principles by which created intelligences can find hope, health, happiness, and heavenly assurance, while living on a planet still to be sanitized from all the evil for which Satan is responsible.

To say it another way, the great controversy is not a spectator sport. It does not give anyone the luxury of sitting in the bleachers. You and I are actors on the stage of the universe. How we play our part will determine not only our eternal futures but also help significantly in vindicating the integrity of God's order in the universe.

Stephen Hawking, that remarkable Cambridge University mathematician and cosmologist, in his 1988 book *A Brief History of Time,* wrote that were scientists to discover the long-sought "theory of everything" to explain the varying mechanisms of the universe, "we would truly know the mind of God."[2] Seventh-day Adventists have been given just that— the "theory of everything," that truly introduces us to the "mind of God." We didn't discover it—it was given to us. We call it the Great Controversy Theme, the unified field of clarity as to what is going on in this wonderful universe.[3]

Here we summarize the overall scope of the Great Controversy Theme (GCT):

> "The **central theme** of the Bible, the theme about which every other in the whole book clusters, is the redemption plan, the **restoration in the human soul of the image of God**. From the first intimation of hope in the sentence pronounced in Eden to that last glorious promise of the Revelation, 'They shall see His face; and His name shall be in their foreheads' (Revelation 22:4), the burden of every book and every passage of the Bible is the unfolding of **this wondrous theme**,—man's uplifting,—the power of God, 'which giveth us the victory through our Lord Jesus Christ.' (1 Corinthians 15:57). He who grasps this thought has before him an infinite field for study. He has **the key** that will unlock to him the whole treasure house of God's word."—*Education,* 125, emphasis supplied).
>
> "The Bible is its own expositor. Scripture is to be compared with scrip-

> ture. The student should learn to **view the word as a whole, and to see the relation of its parts**. He should gain a knowledge of **its grand central theme**, of God's original purpose for the world, of the rise of the great controversy, and of the work of redemption. He should understand the nature of the **two principles that are contending for supremacy**, and should learn to trace their working through the records of history and prophecy, to the great consummation. He should see **how this controversy enters into every phase of human experience**; how in every act of life he himself reveals the one or the other of the two antagonistic motives; and how, whether he will or not, he is **even now deciding upon which side of the controversy he will be found.**"—*Ibid.*, 190 (emphasis supplied).

These are very sobering words, words that must be read often. The GCT is the one theme that fully answers the question: What does God want to accomplish in His Plan of Salvation?

Lucifer (later Satan) was clever and deceitful in charging God as being ultimately self-centered in wanting everything done His way with no "freedom" for independent thinking. Because God didn't grant this new kind of "freedom," Satan pictured God as "severe and unforgiving"—a "being whose chief attribute is stern justice,—one who is a severe judge, a harsh, exacting creditor."[4]

The highest purpose for Jesus to leave heaven and come to earth is to tell the truth about God. In doing so, He shut Satan's mouth, vindicating the eternal fairness, justice, and mercies of God.[5] Watching Calvary, the universe of unfallen beings rejoiced with our Lord's cry, "It is finished"—"Satan was defeated. Not until Christ's death was the character of Satan clearly revealed to the angels or to the unfallen worlds."[6]

But God's plan for our salvation was not, even then, yet complete, either to the unfallen angels or to those on Planet Earth. Even though Satan's disguise was torn away, He "was not destroyed." God knew that more time was needed to get the good news of Calvary out to mankind the world over. If Calvary was total victory for God in the controversy with Satan, God would have declared victory and the millennium would have begun.

But the facts are that "the angels did not even then understand all that was involved in the great controversy. The principles at stake were to be more fully revealed. And for the sake of man, Satan's existence must be continued. Man as well as angels must see the contrast between the Prince of light and the prince of darkness. He must choose whom he will serve."[7]

God, of course, has His plan. Before Jesus ascended He laid out the job description for the Christian Church. John recorded part of our Lord's incredibly moving prayer to His Heavenly Father, wherein Jesus said: "As you

have sent me into the world, I also have sent them into the world" (17:18; see also 20:21).

Obviously, this requires a second reading on our knees. Could He possibly mean what He said? What Jesus was sent into this world to do, so He sends us to do! Could it then be that, in some important aspects, the plan of salvation depends on His disciples doing faithfully what He did so faithfully? And if they do not, they would be His followers in name only! And some day such followers will hear those dreadful words, "I never knew you [for what you said you were]" (Matthew 7:23).

When I read this job description, I see God as our Heavenly Franchiser. He has something special to offer everyone who would "buy" from Him. He offers these franchises freely to all who will commit themselves to represent what He stands for—faithfully, clearly, day in and day out.

Jesus has always found some, in every generation and in all lands, who get the point. They discovered that working for the Heavenly Franchise became their life! Nothing was more exciting! These local franchises know that they are not as perfect as their Head Office. But they also know that if they would keep listening to Headquarters, and stay close to company representatives (who are always on their side to help them reach all expectations), their local franchise will increasingly reflect the original Pattern of the Divine Franchiser.[8]

Why did He make "human beings . . . a new and distinct order"? Because the human family would become one of His best laboratories for the working out of His "side" of the conflict, as well as an open display of how Satan's principles would work out.

This "new and distinct order" of created intelligences was the "talk" of the universe: "All heaven took a deep and joyful interest in the creation of the world and of man. . . . They were made 'in the image of God' and it was the Creator's design that they should populate the earth."[9]

Even further, God had planned that in the development of the human race He would "put it in our power, through co-operation with Him, to bring this scene of misery to an end."[10] That sounds like a lot of responsibility—the capacity to hasten the Advent (or delay it)!

Now, hours before Calvary and only a few weeks before His ascension, Jesus was putting Plan C into action. Plan A failed when Adam and Eve walked out of the Garden. Plan B failed when Israel missed its opportunity to be God's faithful franchise.

And now—the Christian church! Men and women of faith would be-

come His divine franchises throughout the world, building the case that God can be trusted, that He is fair with His laws, that He is merciful beyond words, and that His grace melts our hearts and empowers weak wills so that His will can be done on earth even as it is done by joyful, enthusiastic, compliant angels in heaven (Luke 11:2). "That which God purposed to do for the world through Israel, the chosen nation, He will finally accomplish through His church on earth today."[11]

In Plan C we have the same mission and purpose for the church that God had for Adam and Eve and for the Jewish nation: "Through His people Christ is to manifest His character and the principles of His kingdom. . . . He desires through His people to answer Satan's charges by showing the results of obedience to right principles."[12]

This connection between God's commission to the church—that the Christian's reflection of His character and principles would be His "witness" to the world, and that the return of Jesus depends on when this "witness" has been faithfully done—is neatly summarized in these words:

> "It is the darkness of misapprehension of God that is enshrouding the world. Men are losing their knowledge of His character. It has been misunderstood and misinterpreted. At this time a message from God is to be proclaimed, a message illuminating in its influence and saving in its power. His character is to be made known. Into the darkness of the world is to be shed the light of His glory, the light of His goodness, mercy, and truth. . . . Those who wait for the Bridegroom's coming are to say to the people, 'Behold your God.' The last rays of merciful light, the last message of mercy to be given to the world, is a revelation of His character of love. The children of God are to manifest His glory. In their own life and character they are to reveal what the grace of God has done for them. The light of the Sun of Righteousness is to shine forth in good works—in words of truth and deeds of holiness."[13]

Let's remind ourselves of reality: If Jesus beat Satan at every turn, if all heaven and unfallen worlds saw Satan unmasked when Jesus died,[14] why isn't the controversy over? If Jesus vindicated the character and government of God, what more is needed in order to end the great controversy? If Jesus settled everything in His life and death, why does God stand by and permit the horrors and sadnesses of the past 2000 years? The answer is: something is still unfinished after the cross.

That is why, after Jesus tore the disguise off Satan on Calvary, Jesus then turned to His emerging church as He set up local franchises to continue doing throughout the world what He did for thirty-three years in a very limited area, east of the Mediterranean Sea.

That's why Ellen White sharpens our focus in emphasizing that "the

principles at stake were to be more fully revealed. And for the sake of man, Satan's existence must be continued. Man as well as angels must see the contrast between the Prince of light and the prince of darkness."[15]

In God's infinite wisdom, He put Himself at risk again when He gave to Christians the mission of completing the controversy between Him and Satan. The Christian church is God's Plan C "in the fulfillment of God's great purpose for the human race."[16]

Again, looking at the Big Picture, the Great Controversy theme explains why no one on earth would know what really happened on the cross *unless* "disciples" made it known. Would these "disciples" be believed if the "good news" they talked about did not make a difference in their lives, when compared with others who also had strong religious beliefs in their "gods"? Would anyone really have given Paul any attention if he had not been convinced that the crucified Jesus had indeed come from heaven with God's good news—and that it made a difference? (See Rom. 1:16, 17.)

Again, the Big Picture—God has allowed Himself to be put on trial before the universe.[17] God and the church are both on trial for the same reasons: to prove Satan wrong in all the charges and accusations that he has brought against the character and government of God.

No wonder Ellen White was concerned enough to ask:

> "In this crisis, where is the church to be found? Are its members meeting the claims of God? Are they fulfilling His commission, and representing His character to the world? Are they urging upon the attention of their fellowmen the last merciful message of warning?"[18]

Now the question: Is it possible that professed followers of Jesus Christ could ever be expected to help vindicate God in the great controversy? Everything we have said so far goes a long way toward answering that question. But let's linger at the implications that the question brings up.

Ezekiel in his day was concerned with this question and its answer. He was a captive with many other Israelites in Babylon; for hundreds of years, they had truly become an embarrassment to their Lord, and He could no longer defend them.

In referring to Plan B, God told Ezekiel how Israel had brought dishonor on His name and failed to fulfill their mission:

> "But when they came to the nations, wherever they came, they profaned my holy name, in that men said of them, 'These are the people of the Lord, and yet they had to go out of his land.' But I had concern for my holy name, which the house of Israel caused to be profaned among the nations to which they came. Therefore . . . It is not for your sake, O house of

> Israel, that I am about to act, but for the sake of my holy name, which you have profaned among the nations. . . . And I will vindicate the holiness of my great name, which has been profaned among the nations. . . . and the nations will know that I am the Lord . . .when *through you I vindicate my holiness* before their eyes" (36:20–23, RSV, emphasis supplied).

Our Lord's life and death were one phase of the vindication of God that lies at the heart of the Great Controversy. The second phase of vindicating the name—the character—of God would be lived out through the work of grace in the lives of loyal Christians: "The Savior came to glorify the Father by the demonstration of His love; so the Spirit was to glorify Christ by revealing His grace to the world. The very image of God is to be reproduced in humanity. The honor of God, the honor of Christ, is involved in the perfection of the character of His people."[19]

The character of end-time Christians who "keep the commandments of God and the faith of Jesus" reflects the same quality exhibited in the lives of Enoch, Daniel, and all the others in times past who have let God give them new hearts and new spirits, hearts of flesh instead of hearts of stone.[20]

Job's experience has been the template for faithful men and women: "According to his faith, so was it unto Job. 'When He hath tried me,' he said, 'I shall come forth as gold.' Job 23:10. So it came to pass. By his patient endurance he vindicated his own character, and thus the character of Him whose representative he was."[21]

When we understand that the Christian's highest privilege is to join with Jesus in vindicating the character of God throughout the universe, our whole religious direction is turned upside down. Or is that, right side up? Instead of focusing on self-centered reward and need for constant approval, the deepest impulse becomes one of making the vindication of God, defending the goodness of God, supreme. Such is the gratitude of *agape* love in response to His magnificent love toward us.

Plan C embraces all aspects of the Christian's life. Everything takes on a new color—a new kind of breeze is blowing. A new reason for everything we do becomes clear and motivating. Ellen White's plea echoes throughout her writings:

> "If there was ever a people in need of constantly increasing light from heaven, it is the people that, in this time of peril, God has called to be the depositaries of His holy law, and to vindicate His character before the world. Those to whom has been committed a trust so sacred must be spiritualized, elevated, vitalized, by the truths they profess to believe."[22]

Further, "It becomes every child of God to vindicate His character. You can magnify the Lord; you can show the power of sustaining grace."[23]

And further yet, "God will have a people upon the earth who will vindicate His honor by having respect to all of His commandments; and His commandments are not grievous, not a yoke of bondage."[24]

Would any Christian who understands what Jesus did in the Garden and on the Cross want to do any less? Those who understand how much God needs their witness are on the way to fulfilling God's Plan C.

One last question—how will we know when the controversy is over? Adventists have said for more than a century that Jesus could come in "their" day. Do we give them A+ for zeal but an F for poor theology? Hardly! Why the seeming delay, similar to the Bridegroom who was late for His wedding (Matthew 25:5)? Why was the wedding delayed? Because His bride [God's professed loyalists] had not "made herself ready" (Revelation 19:17).

The short answer is that God is holding back the seven last plagues, waiting for his last-generation loyalists to be worthy of His seal of approval (Revelation 7:1–4).

Yes, God is waiting to give Latter Rain Power to loyalists who would rightly use His power. They are people God will stamp with His signature, seal with His endorsement, because His people can be trusted—because they have let His Spirit mature their characters.

John describes these last-day loyalists as those "having His Father's name written on their foreheads" (Revelation 14:1). They have "follow[ed] the Lamb [Jesus] wherever He goes. . . and in their mouth was found no deceit, for they are without fault before the throne of God" (vss. 4, 5). John, in vision, sees this group before the throne of God and "they shall see His face, and His name shall be on their foreheads" (22:4).

Yes, these are the same last-generation loyalists that Peter foresees:

> "Therefore, since all these things will be dissolved, what manner of persons ought you to be in holy conduct and godliness, looking for and hastening the coming of the day of God, because of which the heavens will be dissolved, being on fire, and the elements will melt with fervent heat?
>
> "Nevertheless we, according to His promise, look for new heavens and a new earth in which righteousness dwells. There, beloved, looking forward to these things, be diligent to be found by Hi in peace, without spot and blameless" (2:11–14).

That is the picture of how the question is answered: What does God want to accomplish in His Plan of Salvation?

Appendix B: Ellen White's Use of Words Such as *Passions, Inclinations, Propensities, Corruptions,* etc.

Ellen G. White (EGW) is not a master of paradoxes. When using *passions* and *propensities,* she uses the words interchangeably in three different contexts, often distinguishing between "higher" and "lower powers" or "passions":

1. To describe passions and propensities that are divinely given to all as part of being human—to be controlled by reason and the Holy Spirit;
2. To describe passions and propensities that are misused by selfish, evil desires and must be "crucified," "discarded," and "separated" from the Christian's life;
3. To emphasize that complete victory over "evil" passions and propensities is possible in this life.

I. Passions and propensities are divinely given:

"You are of that age when the will, the appetite, and the *passions* clamor for indulgence. *God has implanted these in your nature for high and holy purposes. It is not necessary that they should become a curse* to you by being debased."—*Testimonies,* vol. 3, 84.

II. Such divinely given "passions are to be controlled by reason and the Holy Spirit":

"Unfallen Adam's *appetites* and *passions* were under the control of reason."—*Patriarchs and Prophets,* 45. "The body is to be brought into subjection. The *higher powers* of the being are to rule. The *passions* are to be controlled by the will, which is itself to be under the control of God. The kingly power of reason, sanctified by divine grace, is to bear sway in our lives."—*Ministry of Healing,* 130.

"[Paul's] words, his practices, his *passions*—all were brought under the control of the Spirit of God."—*Acts of the Apostles,* 315.

"It is the grace of God that you need in order that your thoughts may

be disciplined to flow in the right channel, that the words you utter may be right words, and that your *passions* and appetites may be subject to the control of reason, and the tongue be bridled against levity and unhallowed censure and faultfinding. . . . Our natural *propensities* must be controlled, or we can never overcome as Christ overcame."—*Testimonies,* vol. 4, 235.

"If they will with faith and courage bring their will in submission to the will of God, he will teach them, and their lives may be like the pure white lily, full of fragrance on the stagnant waters. They must resolve in the strength of Jesus to control inclination and passion, and every day win victories over Satan's temptations. This is the way God has marked out for men to serve his high purposes."—*Signs of the Times,* July 8, 1880.

"The greatest triumph given us by the religion of Christ is control over ourselves. Our *natural propensities must be controlled,* or we can never overcome as Christ overcame.—*Testimonies,* vol. 4, 235.

"The *natural, hereditary traits of the character* need a firm curb, else earnest zeal, good purposes, will run into evil, and the excess of feeling will produce such impressions upon human hearts that they will be carried away by impulse and will allow impressions to become their guide."—*Selected Messages,* bk. 2, 93.

III. EGW often interchanges the meaning of *passion* and *propensity,* especially when considering that both are to be controlled by reason and the higher powers.

"The *lower passions* have their seat in the body and work through it. The words 'flesh' or 'fleshly' or 'carnal lusts' embrace the lower, corrupt nature; *the flesh of itself* cannot act contrary to the will of God. We are commanded to crucify the flesh, with the affections and lusts. How shall we do it? . . . . Put to death the temptation to sin. The corrupt thought is to be expelled. Every thought is to be brought into captivity to Jesus Christ. All animal *propensities* are to be subjected to the higher powers of the soul."—Manuscript 1, 1888, *The Adventist Home,* 127, 128.

Note: This kind of passion or propensity, common to unfallen Adam and to overcoming Christians, must be what EGW understood when she wrote of Jesus:

"The church of Christ is to represent his character. . . . Jesus says, 'For their sakes I sanctify myself, that they also might be sanctified through the truth.' . . .He left the glories of heaven, and clothed his divinity with humanity, and subjected himself to sorrow, and shame, and reproach, abuse, denial, and crucifixion. *Though he had all the strength of the passion of humanity, never did he yield to temptation to do that which was not pure and elevating and ennobling."*—*Signs of the Times,* Nov 21, 1892.

"The lessons of Christ upon the occasion of receiving the children, should leave a deeper impression upon our minds. . . . They may be way-

ward, and possess passions like those of humanity, but this should not deter us from bringing them to Christ. He blessed children that were possessed *of passions like his own.*"—*Signs of the Times,* April 9, 1896.

IV. Certain passions to be cast out, crucified, overcome, etc:

"The only power that can create or perpetuate true peace is the grace of Christ. When this is implanted in the heart, it will cast out the *evil passions* that cause strife and dissension."—*The Desire of Ages,* 302.

"*Unholy passions* must be crucified. They will clamor for indulgence, but God has implanted in the heart high and holy purposes and desires, and these need not be debased. It is only when we refuse to submit to the control 'I can do all things through Christ.' Phil. 4:13."—*Gospel Workers,* 128.

"The *unsanctified will and passions* must be crucified. This may be regarded as a close and severe work. Yet it must be done, or you will hear the terrible sentence from the mouth of Jesus: "Depart." You can do all things through Christ, who strengtheneth you. You are of that age when the will, the appetite, and the *passions clamor for indulgence. God has implanted these in your nature for high and holy purposes.* It is *not necessary that they should become a curse* to you by being debased."—*Testimonies,* vol. 3, 84.

"Our pride, selfishness, *evil passions,* and love of worldly pleasure must all be overcome; therefore God sends us afflictions to test and prove us, and show us that these evils exist in our characters. *We must overcome through His strength and grace* that we may be partakers of the divine nature, having escaped the corruption that is in the world through lust."—*Testimonies,* vol. 3, 115.

"Whatever may be the *evil practice, the master passion* which through long indulgence binds both soul and body, Christ is able and longs to deliver. He will impart life to the soul that is "dead in trespasses." Eph. 2:1. He will *set free* the captive that is held by weakness and misfortune and the chains of sin."—*The Desire of Ages,* 203.

"*Passion of just as base a quality* may be found in the marriage relation as outside of it. . . . It is not pure love which actuates a man to make his wife an instrument to minister to his lust. It is the *animal passions* which clamor for indulgence. . . .Love is a pure and holy principle; but *lustful passion* will not admit of restraint, and will not be dictated to or controlled by reason . . . . The brain nerve power is squandered by men and women, being called into *unnatural action to gratify base passions*; and this hideous monster, base, low passion, assumes the delicate name of love. Many professed Christians who passed before me seemed *destitute of moral restraint*. . . . [The wife] is made an instrument to minister to the gratification of *low, lustful propensities.* And very many women submit to become slaves to *lustful passion*; they do not possess their

bodies in sanctification and honor. . . . but her chaste, dignified, godlike womanhood has been consumed upon *the altar of base passion*; it has been sacrificed to please her husband. . . . No man can truly love his wife when she will patiently submit to become his slave and minister to his *depraved passions*. . . . He doubts her constancy and purity, tires of her, and seeks new objects to arouse and intensify his *hellish passions*. . . . She sees that he is not controlled by conscience or the fear of God; all these sanctified barriers are broken down by *lustful passions*; all that is godlike in the husband is made the servant of low, brutish lust. . . . Shall the wife feel bound to yield implicitly to the demands of her husband, when she sees that nothing *but base passions* control him, and when her reason and judgment are convinced that she does it to the injury of her body, which God has enjoined upon her to possess in sanctification and honor, to preserve as a living sacrifice to God?. . . . It is not pure, holy love which leads the wife to gratify *the animal propensities* of her husband at the expense of health and life. If she possesses true love and wisdom, she will seek to divert his mind from the *gratification of lustful passions* to high and spiritual themes by dwelling upon interesting spiritual subjects. It may be necessary to humbly and affectionately urge, even at the risk of his displeasure, *that she cannot debase her body by yielding to sexual excess*."—*Testimonies,* vol. 2, 474, 475.

"The lust of the eye and *corrupt passions* are aroused by beholding and by reading. The heart is corrupted through the imagination. The mind takes pleasure in contemplating scenes which awaken the *lower and baser passions*. These vile images, seen through defiled imagination, corrupt the morals and prepare the deluded, infatuated beings to give loose rein to *lustful passions*. Then follow sins and crimes which drag beings formed in the image of God down to a level with the beasts, sinking them at last in perdition. Avoid reading and seeing things which will suggest impure thoughts. Cultivate the moral and intellectual powers. Let not these noble powers become enfeebled and perverted by much reading of even storybooks. I know of strong minds that have been unbalanced and partially benumbed, or paralyzed, by intemperance in reading."—*Testimonies,* vol. 2, 410.

"A fearful retribution awaits them, and yet they are controlled by impulse and *gross passion*; they are filling out a dark life record for the judgment. I lift my voice of warning to all who name the name of Christ to depart from all iniquity. *Purify* your souls by obeying the truth. *Cleanse* yourselves from all filthiness of the flesh and spirit, perfecting holiness in the fear of God. You to whom this applies know what I mean."—*Tesiimonies,* vol. 3,475.

"That which ye sow ye shall also reap. These young men are now sowing the seed. Every act of their lives, every word spoken, is a seed for good or evil. As is the seed, so will be the crop. If they indulge *hasty, lustful, perverted passions* or give up to the *gratification of appetite or the inclination* of their unsanctified hearts; if they foster pride or wrong principles and cherish habits of unfaithfulness or dissipation, they will reap

a plentiful harvest of remorse, shame, and despair."—*Testimonies,* vol. 3, 226, 227.

This above list of passions are far different than the passions that are to be controlled: "vicious," "perverted," "murderous," "hasty, lustful," "bitter or baleful," "corrupt," "hellish," "base," "depraved," etc. These passions are to be "overcome," "crucified"—in other words, eliminated. **These are not the passions Jesus ever had— He did not yield nor permit Himself to be corrupted by daily temptation.**

This is why EGW could write in referring to Jesus:

"He was unsullied with corruption, a stranger to sin; yet He prayed, and that often with strong crying and tears. He prayed for His disciples and for Himself, thus identifying Himself with our needs, our weaknesses, and our failings, which are so common with humanity. He was a *mighty petitioner, not possessing the passions of our human, fallen natures, but compassed with like infirmities, tempted in all points even as we are.* Jesus endured agony which required help and support from His Father."—*Testimonies,*vol.2, 508, 509.

"Our Saviour identifies Himself with our needs and weaknesses, in that He became a suppliant, a nightly petitioner, seeking from His Father fresh supplies of strength, to come forth invigorated and refreshed, braced for duty and trial. He is our example in all things. He is a *brother in our infirmities, but not in possessing like passions.* As the sinless One, His nature recoiled from evil."—*Testimonies,* vol. 2, 202.

V. As we did with EGW's use of *passions* to be "crucified," let us now look at her use of *propensities* that must be eliminated from the maturing Christian's life.

"I have been shown that they gratify their *selfish propensities* and do only such things as agree with their tastes and ideas. They make provision for indulgence in pride and sensuality and carry out their selfish ambitions and plans. They are full of self-esteem. But although their *evil propensities* may seem to them as precious as the right hand or the right eye, they *must be separated* from the worker, or he cannot be acceptable before God."—*Testimonies to Ministers,* 171, 172.

"If, like Daniel, young men and young women will bring all their habits, appetites, and *passions* into conformity to the requirements of God, they will qualify themselves for higher work. They should put from their minds all that is cheap and frivolous. *Nonsense and amusement-loving propensities should be discarded,* as out of place in the life and experience of those who are living by faith on the Son of God."—*The Youth's Instructor,* June 22, 1899.

"What cares the vendor of gossip that he defames the innocent? He

will not stay his evil work, though he destroy hope and courage in those who are already sinking under their burdens. He cares only to indulge his *scandal-loving propensity*."—*Testimonies,* vol. 5, 57.

"You are watching with keen business eye the best chance to secure a bargain. This *scheming propensity* has become second nature with you, and you do not see and realize the evil of encouraging it."—*Testimonies,* vol. 4, 351.

"Parents . . . have abused their marriage privileges, and by indulgence have strengthened their *animal passions*. . . . Children are born with *the animal propensities* largely developed, the parents' own stamp of character having been given to them. . . . Those who feel at liberty, because married, to degrade their bodies by beastly indulgence of the animal passions, will have their degraded course perpetuated in their children. The sins of the parents will be visited upon their children because the parents have given them the stamp of their own *lustful propensities*."—*Testimonies,* vol. 2, 391.

VI. EGW never said that all passions and propensities were to be "crucified," or "separated" from the Christian's life—only the "evil" passions and propensities. Why? The natural, God-given passions/propensities obviously will remain and are to remain under control until we are translated or resurrected:

"The training and education of a lifetime must often be discarded that the Christian may become a learner in the school of Christ, and in him who would be a partaker of the divine nature, *appetite and passion must be brought under the control of the Holy Spirit. There is to be no end to this warfare this side of eternity,* but while there are constant battles to fight, there are also precious victories to gain, and the triumph over self and sin is of more value than the mind can estimate. The effort put forth to overcome, though requiring self-denial, is of little account beside the victory over evil."—*Christian Education,* 122; *Counsels to Teachers,* 21.

In other words, not the absence of conflict but the promise of overcoming victory, this side of eternity.

VII. From all the above examples (which are only a few examples and not an exhaustive list), we can better understand EGW when she wrote:

"We must realize that through belief in him it is our privilege to be partakers of the divine nature, and so escape the corruption that is in the world through lust. Then we are cleansed from all sin, all defects of character. *We need not retain one sinful propensity.* Christ is the sin-bearer; John point-

ed the people to him, saying, 'Behold the Lamb of God, which taketh away the sin of the world.' . . . As we partake of the divine nature, *hereditary and cultivated tendencies* to wrong are cut away from the character, and we are made a living power for good."—*Review and Herald,* April 24, 1900.

VIII. And when referring to Jesus, she wrote:

"He took upon Himself human nature, and was tempted in all points as human nature is tempted. He could have sinned; He could have fallen, but *not for one moment was there in Him an evil propensity.* . . . Never, in any way, leave the slightest impression upon human minds that a taint of, or inclination to corruption rested upon Christ, or that He in any way yielded to corruption."—*Manuscript Releases,* vol. 13: 18, 19.

Jesus was at war with all temptations to satisfy His human desires and propensities, which we all have—but He resisted, recoiled, overcame all of them. He overcame these base passions/propensities by the kingly power of reason and the Holy Spirit:

"But here we must not become in our ideas common and earthly, and in our perverted ideas we must not think that the liability of Christ to yield to Satan's temptations degraded His humanity and He possessed the same sinful, corrupt propensities as man. . . . To suppose He was not capable of yielding to temptation places Him where He cannot be a perfect example for man, and the force and the power of this part of Christ's humiliation, which is the most eventful, is no instruction or help to human beings. . . . The divine nature, combined with the human, made Him capable of yielding to Satan's temptations. Here the test to Christ was far greater than that of Adam and Eve, for Christ took our nature, *fallen but not corrupted, and would not be corrupted unless He received the words of Satan in the place of the words of* God. To suppose He was not capable of yielding to temptation places Him where He cannot be a perfect example for man, and the force and the power of this part of Christ's humiliation, which is the most eventful, is no instruction or help to human beings."—*Manuscript Releases,*vol.16, 182.

Jesus did not have "sinful, corrupt propensities as man," not because He was born with this advantage but because He **chose not** to be "sinful, corrupt propensities as man."

Jesus became human as every child does, by human birth. His heredity gave Him all the weaknesses, passions, and propensities common to every human being. **But by choice**, He did not turn those natural weaknesses, passions, and propensities, into evil passions and propensities.

EGW often makes this clear but never clearer than in *The Desire of Ages,* 49—"It would have been an almost infinite humiliation for the Son of God to take man's nature, even when Adam stood in his innocence in Eden. **But**

Jesus accepted humanity when the race had been weakened by four thousand years of sin. **Like every child of Adam** He accepted the results of the working of the great law of heredity. What these results were is shown in the history of His earthly ancestors. **He came with such a heredity** to share our sorrows and temptations, and to give us the example of a sinless life. . . . Yet into the world where Satan claimed dominion God permitted His Son to come, a helpless babe, subject to the weakness of humanity. He permitted Him to meet life's peril in **common with every human soul, to fight the battle as every child of humanity must fight it, at the risk of failure and eternal loss.**"

When EGW wrote that "He could have sinned; He could have fallen, but *not for one moment was there in **Him an evil propensity,***" she was simply saying that "Jesus could have sinned. . . **but** He didn't."

EGW used the same kind of thinking when she wrote: Adam was tempted by the enemy, and he fell. . . . There were in him no corrupt principles, no *tendencies* to evil. **But** when Christ came to meet the temptations of Satan, He bore "the likeness of sinful flesh."—*Signs of the Times*, October 17, 1900.

Appendix C: The Elliptical Nature of Truth.

Ellipse of Truth

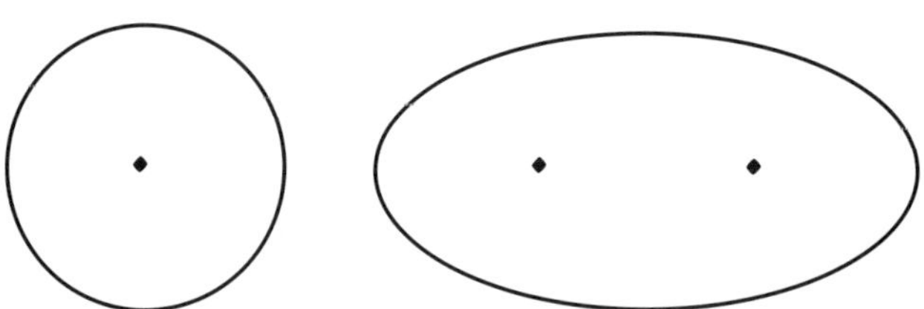

A circle has one focus (center); an ellipse has two focuses (foci).

1. In an ellipse, if the two focuses (foci) separate from each other, we get eventually something like a hotdog! If they get too close to each other, we have made a circle.
2. Either way, we no longer have a true ellipse; items of machinery that use the ellipse principle would suddenly not work if the two foci were moved either closer or farther away.
3. A real ellipse needs both foci to function, with equal emphasis on each, or it ceases to be an ellipse. For example: if we want a glass of water, we don't ask for Hydrogen. Or for Oxygen. To get water, we must create H_20; that is, both Hydrogen and Oxygen are needed in the water ellipse. We can't have one without the other!
4. Theological truths always use the elliptical pattern; for example, God is one focus of the ellipse, and man is the other. In a way, as far as we are concerned, we can't have one without the other.
5. For example, the ellipse of salvation needs grace and faith; if we want salvation, we can't have grace without faith and vice versa.
6. The ellipse of the gospel can be expressed by joining pardon and power; pardon without power to overcome the sin for which we want pardon is only a partial gospel and thus is not what God intended.
7. When we want to understand Christ's role in our salvation, we

note that He is both our Substitute and our Example—we don't have one without the other.

8. When we want to understand Christ's work as our Savior, we see Him on the Cross and we see Him as our High Priest—we don't have one without the other.

Appendix D: "Why Jesus Came the Way He Did."

1. **Jesus came** to be man's Savior and Example—his Substitute and Surety.

"Jesus came down to our world that He might give man a *living example,* required of all—from Adam, the first man, down to the last man who shall live on the earth. . . . He declared that His mission was not to destroy the law but to fill it in perfect and entire obedience. He came to demonstrate the fact that humanity, allied by living faith to divinity, can keep all the commandments of God."—*Review and Herald,* Nov 15, 1898.

"This [sinner's] lamentable condition would have known no change or hope if Jesus had not come down to our world to be *man's Savior and Example.* In the midst of a world's moral degradation, he stands a beautiful and spotless character, the one model for man's imitation. We must study, and copy, and follow the Lord Jesus Christ; then we shall bring the loveliness of his character into our own life, and weave his beauty into our daily words and actions. Thus we shall stand before God with acceptance, and win back by conflict with the principalities of darkness, the power of self-control, and the love of God that Adam lost in the fall. Through Christ we may possess the spirit of love and obedience to the commands of God. Through his merits it may be restored in our fallen natures; and when the Judgment shall sit and the books be opened, we may be the recipients of God's approval."— *Signs of the Times,* Dec 22, 1887.

"When Jesus came to the world it was as our *substitute and surety.* He passed through all the experiences of man, from the manger to Calvary, at every step giving man an example of what he should be and what he should do."—*Signs of the Times,* Apr. 18, 1882.

2. Christ *came to bring divine power to unite with human effort.*

"**Christ came** to bring divine power to unite with human effort, so that although we have been debased by perverted appetite, we may take courage, for we are prisoners of hope. . . .Everyone that is in harmony with Christ will bear the Christ-like mold. . . . **He came** to our world to show us how to live a pure, holy life, and I have purposed in my heart that He shall not have lived and died in vain for me."—*Signs of the Times,* August 4, 1890.

3. Christ came to show mankind how to keep God's law.

"**Christ came** to give an example of the perfect conformity to the law of God required of all—from Adam, the first man, down to the last man who shall live on the earth. He declared that His mission was not to destroy the law but to fill it in perfect and entire obedience. In this way He magnified the law and made it honorable. In His life He revealed its spiritual nature. In the sight of heavenly beings, of worlds unfallen, and of a disobedient, unthankful, unholy world, He fulfilled the far-reaching principles of the law. **He came** to demonstrate the fact that humanity, allied by living faith to divinity, can keep all the commandments of God.

"**He came** to make plain the immutable character of the law, to declare that disobedience and transgression can never be rewarded with eternal life. He came as a man to humanity, that humanity might touch humanity, while divinity laid hold upon the throne of God. But in no case did he come to lessen the obligation of men to be perfectly obedient. He did not destroy the validity of the Old Testament Scriptures. He fulfilled that which was predicted by God himself. He came, not to set men free from that law, but to open a way whereby they might obey that law, and teach others to do the same."—*Review and Herald,* November 15, 1898.

4. Jesus came not only to atone for sin, but also to be a teacher both by precept and example. He came to show man how to keep the law in humanity.

"**The great Teacher came** into our world, not only to atone for sin, but to be a teacher both by precept and example. He came to show man how to keep the law in humanity, so that man might have no excuse for following his own defective judgment. We see Christ's obedience. His life was without sin. His life-long obedience is a reproach to disobedient humanity. The obedience of Christ is not to be put aside as altogether different from the obedience He requires of us individually. Christ has shown us that it is possible for all humanity to obey the laws of God. He served as a son with the Father. Just so we must every one serve with God, not in our own improvised plans"—*Selected Messages,* bk. 3: 135, 136.

5. Jesus came to our world, not to reveal what a God could do, but what a man could do, through faith in God's power to help in every emergency.

"The Lord **Jesus came** to our world, not to reveal what a God could do, but what a man could do, through faith in God's power to help in every emergency. Man is, through faith, to be a partaker in the divine

nature, and to overcome every temptation wherewith he is beset. The Lord now demands that every son and daughter of Adam through faith in Jesus Christ, serve Him in human nature which we now have."—Manuscript 1, 1892, printed in *Review and Herald,,* June 17, 1976.

6. Christ came that He might recreate the image of God in man.

"**Jesus came** to our world to bring divine power to man, that through his grace, we might be transformed into His likeness."—*Signs of the Times,* June 16, 1890.

"The contemplation of the love of God manifested in His Son will stir the heart and arouse the powers of the soul as nothing else can. **Christ came** that He might re-create the image of God in man; and whoever turns men away from Christ is turning them away from the source of true development; he is defrauding them of the hope and purpose and glory of life."—*The Desire of Ages,* 478.

He **came** to restore in man the defaced image of God, to impart to the repentant soul divine power by which he might be raised from corruption and degradation, and be elevated and ennobled and made fit for companionship with the angels of heaven.—*Review and Herald,* May 8, 1894.

7. Christ came to this world and lived the law of God, that man might have perfect mastery over the natural inclinations that corrupt the soul.

"Not until the life of Christ becomes a vitalizing power in our lives can we resist the temptations that assail us from within and from without. **Christ came** to this world and lived the law of God, that man might have perfect mastery over the natural inclinations which corrupt the soul. The Physician of soul and body, He gives victory over warring lusts. He has provided every facility, that man may possess completeness of character."—*The Ministry of Healing,* 130–132.

"**Christ came** to cut us loose from the originator of sin. He came to give us a mastery over the power of the destroyer, and to save us from the sting of the serpent. Through his imparted righteousness he would place all human beings where they will be on vantage ground. He came to this earth and lived the law of God that man might stand in his God-given manhood, having complete mastery over his natural inclination to self-indulgence and to the selfish ideas and principles which tarnish the soul. The Physician of soul and body, he will give wisdom and complete victory over warring lusts. He will provide every facility, that man may perfect a completeness of character in every respect"—*Manuscript Releases* 7, 320.

8. **Christ came** to the earth, not merely that the inhabitants of this little world might regard the law of God as it should be regarded. but to vindicate the character of God before the universe.

> "The plan of salvation had a yet broader and deeper purpose than the salvation of man. It was not for this alone that **Christ came** to the earth; it was not merely that the inhabitants of this little world might regard the law of God as it should be regarded; but it was to vindicate the character of God before the universe."—*Patriarchs and Prophets,* 68.

9. Christ came in the form of humanity, and by His perfect obedience He proved that humanity and divinity combined can obey every one of God's precepts.

> "Satan had claimed that it was impossible for man to obey God's commandments; and in our own strength it is true that we can not obey them. But **Christ came** in the form of humanity, and by His perfect obedience He proved that humanity and divinity combined can obey every one of God's precepts."—*Christ's Object Lessons,* 314.

> "**Christ came** to the world to counteract Satan's falsehood that God had made a law which men could not keep. Taking humanity upon Himself, He came to this earth, and by a life of obedience showed that God has not made a law that man cannot keep. He showed that it is possible for man perfectly to obey the law. Those who accept Christ as their Savior, becoming partakers of His divine nature, are enabled to follow His example, living in obedience to every precept of the law. Through the merits of Christ, man is to show by his obedience that he could be trusted in heaven, that he would not rebel."—*The Faith I Live By,* 114.

> "To attribute to his nature a power that it is not possible for man to have in his conflicts with Satan, is to destroy the completeness of his humanity. The obedience of Christ to his Father was the same obedience that is required of man. Man cannot overcome Satan's temptations except as divine power works through humanity. The Lord **Jesus came** to our world, not to reveal what God in his own divine person could do, but what he could do through humanity. Through faith man is to be a partaker of the divine nature, and to overcome every temptation wherewith he is beset. It was the Majesty of heaven who became a man, who humbled himself to our human nature; it was he who was tempted in the wilderness and who endured the contradiction of sinners against himself."—*Signs of the Times,* April 10, 1893.

> "Christ came to this world to show that by receiving power from on high, man can live an unsullied life."—*The Ministry of Healing,* 25.

10. Christ came to set aside the false teaching by which those who claimed to know God had misrepresented Him.

"**[Christ] came** to set aside the false teaching by which those who claimed to know God had misrepresented Him. He came to manifest the nature of the law, to reveal in His own character the beauty of holiness. . . . Sweeping away the exactions which had encumbered the law of God, He showed that the law is a law of love, an expression of the Divine Goodness. He showed that in obedience to its principles is involved the happiness of mankind, and with it the stability, the very foundation and framework, of human society. . . .So far from making arbitrary requirements, God's law is given to men as a hedge, a shield. . . . **Christ came** to demonstrate the value of the divine principles by revealing their power for the regeneration of humanity. He came to teach how these principles are to be developed and applied."—*Education,* 76, 77.

11. Jesus came to impart to the human soul the Holy Spirit by which the love of God is shed abroad in the heart; but it is impossible to endow men with the Holy Spirit, who are set in their ideas.

"**Jesus came** to impart to the human soul the Holy Spirit by which the love of God is shed abroad in the heart; but it is impossible to endow men with the Holy Spirit, who are set in their ideas, whose doctrines are all stereotyped and unchangeable, who are walking after the traditions and commandments of men as were the Jews in the time of Christ. They were very punctilious in the observance of the church, very rigorous in following their forms, but they were destitute of vitality and religious devotion."—*Manuscript Releases,* 52.

12. Jesus came to tell the truth about God.

"Christ exalted the character of God, attributing to him the praise and giving to him the credit, of the **whole purpose of his own mission on earth,—to set men right through the revelation of God**. In Christ was arrayed before men the paternal grace and the matchless perfections of the Father. In his prayer just before His crucifixion, he declared, 'I have manifested thy name.' 'I have glorified thee on the earth; I have finished the work which thou gavest me to do.' When the object of his mission was attained, the Son of God announced that his work was accomplished, and that the character of the Father was made manifest to men."—*Signs of the Times,* Jan. 20, 1890.

"When the world was destitute of the knowledge of God, **Jesus came** to impart this inestimable blessing—a knowledge of the paternal character of our heavenly Father. This was His own gift to our world; and this gift He committed to His disciples, to be communicated by them to the world."—*Testimonies to Ministers,* 193.

"Everyone who is chosen of God should improve his intellectual powers. **Jesus came** to represent the character of the Father, and He sent His disciples into the world to represent the character of Christ. He has given us His word to point out the way of life, and He has not left us simply to carry that word, but has also promised to give it efficiency by the power of the Holy Spirit."—*Testimonies to Ministers,* 199.

13. He came not to save us in our sins, but from our sins.

"Christ would not have come to this earth if the commandments had not been broken. **He came** not to save us in our sins, but from our sins. There is no true happiness in transgression, but in obedience. Our merit is in the blood of Christ. But men think they can transgress and shun the cross, and yet enter into the city."—*Manuscript Releases* 3, 98.

"**Jesus came** not to save men in their sins, but from their sins. 'Sin is the transgression of the law,' and if we fail to obey the law, we do not accept our Saviour. The only hope we have of salvation is through Christ. If his Spirit abides in the heart, sin cannot dwell there."—*Review and Herald,* March 16, 1886.

"**Jesus came** into the world to save sinners, not in their sins but from their sins, and to sanctify the truth; and in order that he may become a perfect Saviour to us, we must enter into union with him by a personal act of faith. Christ has chosen us, we have chosen him, and by this choice we become united to him, and are to live from henceforth, not unto ourselves, but unto him who has died for us."—*Signs of the Times,* March 23, 1888 par. 2.

14. He came to this earth, suffered, and knows just how to sympathize with us and to assist us in overcoming.

"Christ knew that man could not overcome without His help. Therefore He consented to lay off His royal robes and clothe His divinity with humanity that we might be rich. **He came to this earth**, suffered, and knows just how to sympathize with us and to assist us in overcoming. **He came** to bring man moral power, and He would not have man to understand that he has nothing to do, for every one has a work to do for himself, and through the merits of Jesus we can overcome sin and the devil."—3MR 108.

"**The Redeemer of the world came** from heaven to help man in his weakness, that, in the power which **Jesus came** to bring him, he might become strong to overcome appetite and passion and might be victor on every point."—*Counsels on Health,* 125.

15. The world's Redeemer came not only to be a sacrifice for sin but to be an example to man in a holy human character.

    "**Jesus came** to our world to perfect a Christian character in behalf of the fallen race— the requirement of God to us is to practice the example of our Substitute and Surety"—*Manuscript Releases* 20, 282.

16. Jesus came to show us that a lifelong obedience is possible.

    "We are ever to be thankful that Jesus has proved to us by actual facts that man can keep the commandments of God, giving contradiction to Satan's falsehood that man cannot keep them. The **Great Teacher came** to our world to stand at the head of humanity, to thus elevate and sanctify humanity by His holy obedience to all of God's requirements showing it is possible to obey all the commandments of God. He had demonstrated that a lifelong obedience is possible."—Ms 1, 1892, 1, 2, 6, 7, 8; *Manuscript Releases* 5, 113.

17. Jesus gave us an example of how to overcome sin.

    "We should put forth every effort to overcome evil. **Christ came** to set us an example of how to overcome. . . . Our characters are photographed on the books of heaven, and from these books we are to be judged."—*Manuscript Releases* 3, 116.

    "**He came** to earth to unite his divine power with our human efforts, that **through the strength and moral power which he imparts, we may overcome in our own behalf."**—*Signs of the Times*, Aug. 7, 1879.

    "As we see the condition of mankind today, the question arises in the minds of some, "Is man by nature totally and wholly depraved?" Is he hopelessly ruined? No, he is not. **The Lord Jesus left the royal courts and, taking our human nature, lived such a life as everyone may live in humanity, through following His example.** We may perfect a life in this world [which] is an example of righteousness, and overcome as Christ has given us an example in His life, revealing that humanity may conquer as He, the great Pattern, [conquered]. Men have sold themselves to the enemy of all righteousness. **Christ came to our world to live the example humanity must live, if they [are to] secure the heavenly reward. . . .Christ lived the unpolluted life in this world to reveal to human beings the power of His grace** that will be given to every soul that will accept Him as his Saviour."—*Manuscript Releases* 9, 239.

18. Jesus came to show us self-sacrifice and self-denial.

"The true spirit of the Christian religion is one of self-sacrifice; self-denial is required at every step. **Jesus came** down from Heaven to teach us how to live; and his life was one of toil and self-denial."—*Signs of the Times,* April 21, 1887.

19. Jesus came to bring mankind moral power.

"Jesus came to this earth, marred and seared by the curse, for the purpose of bringing moral power to men. He fought the battle in man's behalf in the wilderness of temptation, and it was the same battle that everyone of us must fight till the close of time."—*Signs of the Times,* September 30, 1889.

"Do not continue to talk of your weakness; **Jesus came** to bring moral power to combine with human effort, that we might advance step by step in the heavenward way. Let your faith lay hold of the precious promises of God, and if clouds have encompassed you, the mists will roll back; for the angels of God are ever ready to help in every trial and emergency. We are not left to battle unaided against the prince of darkness."—*Bible Echo,* December 1, 1892.

"The young may have moral power, for **Jesus came** into the world that He might be our example and give to all youth and those of every age divine help."—*Child Guidance,* 167.

"The Lord Jesus **came to our world to represent the Father**. He represented God not as an essence that pervaded nature, but as a God who has a personality. Christ was the express image of His Father's person; and He came to our world **to restore in man God's moral image, in order that man, although fallen, might through obedience to God's commandments become enstamped** with the divine image and character--adorned with the beauty of divine loveliness."—*Manuscript Releases* 9, 250.

20. Christ came to show the purpose of the Christian Church.

"The formation of the Christian church, and the union of all that it embraces, and preserving the consecration of all its powers as the appointed agencies of God, for the **spiritual recovery of the moral image of God in man, was the object of Christ assuming human nature**. Christ was the foundation of the whole Jewish economy, which was the symbol prescribed in type for the religious faith and obedience of all people."—*Manuscript Releases* 9, 333.

21. Jesus came to unmask the deceiver.

"In heaven Satan had declared that the sin of Adam revealed that human beings could not keep the law of God, and he sought to carry the universe with him in this belief. Satan's words appeared to be true, but **Christ came to unmask the deceiver**. He came that through trial and dispute of the claims of Satan in the great conflict, He might demonstrate that a ransom had been found. The Majesty of heaven would undertake the cause of man, and with the same facilities that man may obtain, stand the test and proving of God as man must stand it.

. . . .**Christ came** to the earth, taking humanity and standing as man's representative, to show in the controversy with Satan that he was a liar, and that man, as God created him, connected with the Father and the Son, could obey every requirement of God. Speaking through His servant He declares, 'His commandments are not grievous.' It was sin that separated man from his God, and it is sin that maintains this separation."—*Manuscript Releases* 15, 115.

22. Jesus came as our substitute and surety so that we might be overcomers with Him.

"Christ ventured a great deal when He came here to stand upon the battlefield, when He came here clothed with humanity**, standing as our surety, as our substitute, that He would overcome in our behalf, that we might be overcomers in His strength and by His merits.**"—*Manuscript Releases* 9, 52.

"When **Jesus came** to the world it was as our substitute and surety. He passed through all the experiences of man, from the manger to Calvary, at every step giving man an example of what he should be and what he should do."—*Signs of the Times,* April 18, 1892.

23. Jesus is the only way for us to understand the meaning of justification and sanctification.

"**Christ came** to save fallen man, and Satan with fiercest wrath met him on the field of conflict; for the enemy knew that when divine strength was added to human weakness, man was armed with power and intelligence, and could break away from the captivity in which he had bound him. . . . God was represented as severe, exacting, revengeful, and arbitrary. He was pictured as one who could take pleasure in the sufferings of his creatures. The very attributes that belonged to the character of Satan, the evil one represented as belonging to the character of God. **Jesus came** to teach men of the Father, to correctly represent him before the fallen children of earth. . . . **The only way in which he could set and keep men right was to**

make himself visible and familiar to their eyes. That men might have salvation he came directly to man, and became a partaker of his nature. . . . After the plan of salvation was devised, Satan could have no ground upon which to found his suggestion that God, because so great, could care nothing for so insignificant a creature as man. The redemption of man is a wonderful theme, and the love manifested to the fallen race through the plan of salvation, can be estimated only by the cross of Calvary."—*Signs of the Times,* Jan. 20, 1890.

24. Jesus came to impart His righteousness.

"Jesus came to suffer in our behalf, that He might impart to us His righteousness. There is but one way of escape for us, and that is found only in becoming partakers of the divine nature."—*Selected Messages,* bk. 3, 197.

" He lived the law of God, and honored it in a world of transgression, revealing to the worlds unfallen, to the heavenly universe, to Satan, and to all the fallen sons and daughters of Adam that through His grace humanity can keep the law of God! **He came to impart** His own divine nature, His own image, to the repentant, believing soul."—*Manuscript Releases* 8, 40.

Appendix E: "Why Jesus Died."

Satan loves to use such words as *gospel, forgiveness, justification,* etc. And phrases such as *Jesus died to save me,* or *Jesus died so that He could forgive my sins.* Why? Because *his definitions* for these biblical words and his explanation for why Jesus died provide the basis for a limited gospel.

To illustrate, *Time,* April 1, 2002, had a cover story entitled, "Can the Catholic Church Save Itself?" Under the section, "The Confession of Father X" were these words of Father X, who was describing his life of lust with young people in his parish: "I'd go to confession; there would be genuine repentance [remorse, but hardly "change of mind"]; and then I would go for a period of time without molesting anyone. I would make a very real point when this was having to be confessed to go to another diocese to make sure the priest didn't know me. What I was after was the absolution, so that I could pick up the pieces and go on."

These may be the words of an unfortunate Catholic priest. But he mirrors all of us when we have Satan's picture of why Jesus died in our heads instead of the big picture within the "everlasting gospel" that God wants made clear in these end times. For too long the Christian churches have lived in the fog of partial truth.

Satan's picture runs something like this: "We are all sinners. We will be sinners until Jesus comes, and if we die before He returns, He will remember that we were sorry for our sins."[25] And continuing, "Didn't Jesus die to cover my sins, and if I ask Him to forgive me, isn't that the good news?"

If this is all we understand as to why Jesus died, then we are believing in Satan's "good news." But that is one of his monstrous lies—again, taking truth and clouding it!

As in all biblical issues, we must keep the big picture in view: the great controversy is focused on vindicating God's fairness and justice in His dealing with His created beings. Satan has accused God of being unfair in making laws that could not be kept and said that if anyone tried, they would be unhappy legalists. But Jesus and His followers prove Satan wrong, exposing his lies as pure sour grapes

First, Jesus earned the right, by His life and death, to forgive sincere-

ly repentant people because He proved in His humanity that God's laws could be cheerfully obeyed, thus satisfying God's justice.[26] In addition, He earned the right to forgive the truly repentant because his or her faith in Him contained the seed of future loyalty and obedient— that same faith that kept Him from sinning.

Second, He earned the right to be our High Priest, who promises to make available "grace to help in time of need" (Heb. 4:16).

Simply put, Jesus lived and died to give us both pardon and power. To ask for His pardon and not His power is to miss the point of why He died. To think that forgiveness is the major or only reason for the death of Jesus is to discover yet another example of the limited gospel.

Augustus Toplady said it well in his beloved hymn, "Rock of Ages" (emphasis added):

"Rock of Ages, cleft for me,
Let me hide myself in Thee;
Let the water and the blood,
From Thy riven side which flowed,
Be of sin the *double cure,*
Cleanse me from *its guilt and power.*"

Let us look at how Ellen White illuminated "the double cure," with the cherished biblical promises that build on why Jesus died (some quotations bridge more than one category):

I. Jesus satisfied "justice," demonstrating that God was indeed "just" in that He did not require the impossible from His created beings:

> "By His life on earth He honored the law of God. By His death He established it. He gave His life as a sacrifice, not to destroy God's law, not to create a lower standard, but that justice might be maintained, that the law might be shown to be immutable, that it might stand fast forever. Satan had claimed that it was impossible for man to obey God's commandments; and in our own strength it is true that we cannot obey them. But Christ came in the form of humanity, and by His perfect obedience He proved that humanity and divinity combined can obey every one of God's precepts."—*Christ's Object Lessons,* 314.

II. Jesus paid the price that shut Satan's mouth regarding whether God could love sinners so much as to suffer the enormous indignities of the cross in order to reconcile us to Him (John 3:16).

1. "All heaven triumphed in the Saviour's victory. Satan was defeated,

and knew that his kingdom was lost. To the angels and the unfallen worlds the cry, 'It is finished,' had a deep significance. It was for them as well as for us that the great work of redemption had been accomplished. They with us share the fruits of Christ's victory. Not until the death of Christ was the character of Satan clearly revealed to the angels or to the unfallen worlds."—*The Desire of Ages,* 758.

2. "Not because we first loved Him, does God love us; but 'while we were yet sinners' (Rom. 5:8) Christ died for us, making full and abundant provision for our redemption."—*Amazing Grace,* 10.

3. "Such is the value of men for whom Christ died that the Father is satisfied with the infinite price which He pays for the salvation of man in yielding up His own Son to die for their redemption. What wisdom, mercy, and love in its fullness are here manifested! The worth of man is known only by going to Calvary. In the mystery of the cross of Christ we can place an estimate upon man."—*Amazing Grace,* 175

4. "By His life and His death, Christ proved that God's justice did not destroy His mercy, but that sin could be forgiven, and that the law is righteous, and can be perfectly obeyed. Satan's charges were refuted. God had given man unmistakable evidence of His love."—*The Desire of Ages,* 762.

III. Jesus suffered the wrath of God [awfulness of being God-forsaken] against transgression.

- "God suffered His wrath against transgression to fall on His beloved Son. Jesus was to be crucified for the sins of men. What suffering, then, would the sinner bear who continued in sin? All the impenitent and unbelieving would know a sorrow and misery that language would fail to express."—*The Desire of Ages,* 743.

IV. In proving Satan wrong and God right, in our Lord's life and death, Jesus earned the victor's right to be our Savior and High Priest.

- "Some by their impenitence would make it an impossibility for the prayer of Christ to be answered for them. Yet, just the same, God's purpose was reaching its fulfillment. Jesus was earning the right to become the advocate of men in the Father's presence."—*The Desire of Ages,* 744.

V. Jesus died to demonstrate the character of God and the value of mankind.

1. "The Lord our Redeemer had not yet demonstrated fully that love to its completeness. After His condemnation in the judgment hall, His crucifixion on the cross, when He cried out in a clear, loud voice, 'It is finished,' that love stands forth as an exhibition of a new love—'as I have loved you'--is demonstrated. Can the human mind take this in? Can we obey the commandment given."—*Manuscript Releases* 16, 190.
2. "Christ died to bring life and immortality to light through the gospel, and therefore man is of value in God's sight."—*Manuscript Releases* 17, 198.
3. "And the Son of God endured this shame as the penalty of guilt, in order that the sinner may stand guiltless and innocent before the throne of God. See what may arise from the height of exaltation from which our Saviour came, and the depth of humiliation to which He reached in order to grasp the sinner and lift him up to become a partaker of His divine nature, and link his life, his soul, with the Infinite God. When we obtain a sight of that cross; when that suffering, agonized cry, "It is finished," pierces our ears, the sacrifice is complete. His love has imprinted the name of every saint upon the palms of His hands."—*Manuscript Releases* 18, 19.

VI. Christ died to reclaim this earth from the usurped authority of Satan.

- "It was to make an inroad on the territory of Satan, and dispute his usurped authority, and reclaim the kingdom unto Himself that Christ died. With the shout of a monarch who has clothed himself with zeal as a cloak, will He fight His antagonist, the prince of darkness, and win back the kingdom Satan claims as his own rightful dominion."—*Manuscript Releases* 18, 54.

VII. Jesus died to underscore the immutability of the law of God—that it could not and should not be altered to fit the whims of created intelligences (Matthew 5:17, 18).

1. "The light that I have is that God's servants should go quietly to work, preaching the grand, precious truths of the Bible—Christ and Him crucified, His love and infinite sacrifice—showing that

the reason why Christ died is because the law of God is immutable, unchangeable, eternal."—*The Southern Work*, 69.

2. "Christ died because there was no other hope for the transgressor. He might try to keep God's law in the future; but the debt which he had incurred in the past remained, and the law must condemn him to death. Christ came to pay that debt for the sinner which it was impossible for him to pay for himself. Thus, through the atoning sacrifice of Christ, sinful man was granted another trial."—*Faith and Works*, 30.

3. "When Christ died, the destruction of Satan was made certain. But if the law was abolished at the cross, as many claim, then the agony and death of God's dear Son were endured only to give to Satan just what he asked; then the prince of evil triumphed, his charges against the divine government were sustained. The very fact that Christ bore the penalty of man's transgression is a mighty argument to all created intelligences that the law is changeless; that God is righteous, merciful, and self-denying; and that infinite justice and mercy unite in the administration of His government."—*Patriarchs and Prophets*, 70.

4. "By the crucifixion of Christ the immutability of the law of God was forever established. He was the Son of God, and had it been possible, God would have changed the law to meet man in his fallen state. But the law of God is unalterable, and the only way that man could be saved was for a Substitute to be provided, who would bear the penalty of transgression, and thus give man an opportunity to return to his loyalty."—*Manuscript Releases* 18, 70.

5. "The reason why Christ died is because the law of God is immutable, unchangeable, eternal."—*Maranatha*,177.

VIII. Because God will not take rebels back into heaven, Christ died to make it possible for sinners to choose loyalty and become obedient commandment-keepers by His promised grace.

1. "Christ died that the transgressor of the law of God might be brought back to His loyalty, that He might keep the commandments of God, and His law as the apple of His eye, and live. God cannot take rebels into His kingdom; therefore He makes obedience to His requirements a special requirement."—*Child Guidance*, 257.

2. "By giving His life for the life of men, He would restore in

humanity the image of God. He would lift us up from the dust, reshape the character after the pattern of His own character, and make it beautiful with His own glory."—*The Ministry of Healing,* 504.

3. "Is the matter of gaining eternal life one to be trifled with? With His own life Christ paid the price of our redemption. He died to secure our love and willing obedience."—*Manuscript Releases* 18, 269.
4. "He died to make it possible for us to keep the law. But all are left to make their choice for themselves. God forces no one to accept the advantages secured for him at an infinite cost."—*The Youth's Instructor,* March 20, 1902.

IX. Christ died because of sin on Planet Earth—the transgression of God's Law.

- "Why did He die? In consequence of sin. What is sin? The transgression of the law. Then the eyes are open to see the character of sin. The law is broken, but cannot pardon the transgressor. It is our schoolmaster, condemning to punishment. Where is the remedy? The law drives us to Christ, who was hanged upon the cross that He might be able to impart His righteousness to fallen, sinful man and thus present men to His Father in His righteous character."—*Seventh-day Adventist Bible Commentary* 1110 (334).

X. Jesus died to provide the basis and purpose for the everlasting gospel—that sinners would take courage and understand the divine power available and live as loyal followers, again proving Satan wrong about the willingness and ability of created beings to obey God (Philippians 2:12–15).

1. "The precious revelation of God's will in the Scriptures with all their unfolding of glorious truth is only a means to an end. The death of Jesus Christ was a means to an end. The most powerful and efficacious provision that He could give to our world, was the means; the end was the glory of God in the uplifting, refining, ennobling of the human agent."—*Manuscript Releases* 7, 274.
2. "Jesus died that He might purify us from all iniquity. The Lord will carry on this work of perfection for us if we will allow ourselves

to be controlled by Him. He carries on this work for our good and His own name's glory."—*Manuscript Releases* 4: 348, 1898.

3. "We hear many excuses; I cannot live up to this or that. What do you mean by this or that? Do you mean that it was an imperfect sacrifice that was made for the fallen race upon Calvary, that there is not sufficient grace and power granted us that we work away from our own natural defects and tendencies, that it was not a whole Saviour that was given us? or do you mean to cast reproach upon God?"—Ms 8, 1888, sermon preached at Minneapolis General Conference, Sabbath, Oct 20, 1888, cited in Olson, *Through Crisis to Victory,* 261, 262.

4. "How could he give you any stronger evidence of his love than he gave when he died for you on Calvary's cross? He died that you might have power to break with Satan that you might cast off his hellish shackles, and be delivered from his power?"—*The Youth Instructor,* March 2, 1893.

5. "Christ died that His life might be lived in you, and in all who make Him their example. In the strength of your Redeemer you can reveal the character of Christ, and you can work in wisdom and in power to make the crooked places straight."—*Gospel Workers,* 164.

6. "By dying on the cross Christ gave His life as an offering for sin, that through His power man might turn from his sins, become converted, and be a laborer together with God."—*Manuscript Releases* 18, 75.

7. "All heaven is interested in the restoration of the moral image of God in man. All heaven is working to this end. God and the holy angels have an intense desire that human beings shall reach the standard of perfection which Christ died to make it possible for them to reach."— *In Heavenly Places,* 286.

8. "When tempted and tried, he claims the power that Christ died to give, and overcomes through His grace. This every sinner needs to understand. He must repent of his sin, he must believe in the power of Christ, and accept that power to save and to keep him from sin."—*Selected Messages,* bk. 1, 224.

9. "We are not, because Christ died, left a company of orphans. . . . It is possible for us to obtain victory after victory, and be the most happy people on the face of the earth."—*Our High Calling,* 148.

10. "But men have been satisfied with small attainments. They have

not sought with all their might to rise in mental, moral, and physical capabilities. They have not felt that God required this of them; they have not realized that Christ died that they might do this very work. As the result they are far behind what they might be in intelligence and in the ability to think and plan."—*Testimonies,* vol. 5, 554.

11. "Christ died that the moral image of God might be restored in humanity, that men and women might be partakers of the divine nature, having escaped the corruption that is in the world through lust. We are to use no power of our being for selfish gratification; for all our powers belong to Him, and are to be used to His glory."—*Review and Herald,* November 6, 1900.

12. "By transgression man was severed from God, the communion between them was broken, but Jesus Christ died upon the cross of Calvary, bearing in His body the sins of the whole world; and the gulf between heaven and earth was bridged by that cross. Christ leads men to the gulf, and points to the bridge by which it is spanned, saying, "If any man will come after me, let him deny himself, and take up his cross daily, and follow me." God gives us a probation in which we may prove whether or not we will be loyal to Him."—Manuscript 21, 1895, cited in *Seventh-day Adventist Bible Commentary,* vol. 7, 465.

13. "Christ died to make an atoning sacrifice for our sins. At the father's right hand He is interceding for us as our High Priest. By the sacrifice of His life He purchased redemption for us. His atonement is effectual for everyone who will humble himself, and receive Christ as his example in all things. If the Saviour had not given His life as a propitiation for our sins, the whole human family would have perished. They would have had no right to heaven. It is through His intercession that we, through faith, repentance, and conversion, are enabled to become partakers of the divine nature, and thus escape the corruption that is in the world through lust."—Manuscript 29, 1906, cited in *Seventh-day Adventist Bible Commentary,* vol. 7, 477.

14. "Christ has died that we might keep God's commandments. Will you have your names registered in the Lamb's book of life? Then be careful and zealous to repent of every sin. He says, 'I will not blot out your name from the book of life, but I will confess it before My Father and His angels' (Revelation 3:5)."—*Manuscript Releases* 9, 264.

15. "When Christ gave His life for you, it was that He might place you on vantage ground and impart to you moral power. By faith you may become partakers of His divine nature, having overcome the corruption that is in the world through lust."—*Manuscript Releases* 14, 73.

16. "Christ came to our world to elevate humanity, to renew in man the image of God, that man might become the partaker of the divine nature. . . .The Majesty of heaven gave His life to make us individually His own by bringing back the transgressor to his loyalty to God's law, by turning away the sinner from his iniquity. Oh, that men would love and fear God!"—*Manuscript Releases* 14, 85.

17. "By the death of His only begotten Son, God has made it possible for man to reach the high ideal set before him. We can do God no greater dishonor than to remain in indolence and indifference, caring not to save the souls perishing in sin."—*Manuscript Releases* 16, 342.

18. "He died that you might be led to see the sinfulness of sin and come unto Him that you might have life."—*Manuscript Releases* 17, 49.

19. "Do not disappoint the One who gave His life that you might be an overcomer. He was tempted on every point that you and I can be tempted on, and in order to resist He spent whole nights in prayer and communion with his Father. Christ did not leave this world until He had made it possible for every soul to live a life of perfect faith and obedience, to have a perfect character."—*Manuscript Releases* 17, 85.

20. "You are not called upon to fast forty days. The Lord bore that fast for you in the wilderness of temptation. There would be no virtue in such a fast; but there is virtue in the blood of Christ. Will you not believe that there is power in His sacrifice to purify and refine you, power in His grace to make you a laborer together with God?"—*Manuscript Releases* 17, 86.

21. "Those who keep the commandments of God should make it manifest that the truth is sanctifying the soul, refining and purifying the thoughts, and elevating the character and life. Christ has died that the moral image of God might be restored in our souls and might be reflected to those around us."—*Faith and Works,* 61.

22. "The cross of Calvary challenges, and will finally vanquish every earthly and hellish power. In the cross all influence centers, and

from it all influence goes forth. It is the great center of attraction; for on it Christ gave up His life for the human race. This sacrifice was offered for the purpose of restoring man to his original perfection. Yea, more, it was offered to give him an entire transformation of character, making him more than a conqueror."—*Seventh-day Adventist Bible Commentary,* vol. 6, 1113.

23. "As a divine Saviour, Jesus died for us that we might live His life of purity, truth, and righteousness. He teaches us how to live. Our prayer should be, "Create in me a clean heart, O God; and renew a right spirit within me."—*Manuscript Releases* 18, 277.

24. "Christ died to save sinners, not in their sins, but from their sins."—*Manuscript Releases* 19, 182.

25. "By dying on the cross Christ gave His life as an offering for sin, that through His power man might turn from his sins, become converted, and be a laborer together with God."—*Manuscript Releases* 18, 75.

26. "As a divine Saviour, Jesus died for us so that we might live His life of purity, truth and righteousness. He teaches us how to live. Our prayer should be, 'Created in me a clean heart, O God; and renew a right spirit within me." —*Manuscript Releases* 18, 277.

27. "The Son of God consented to die in the sinner's stead, that man might, by a life of obedience, escape the penalty of the law."—*Signs of the Times,* Aug 7, 1879.

Appendix F: "What Do We Mean By Moral Perfection in Contrast to Perfectionism?"

Perfection, as used in this book, refers to the *dynamic* life pattern of persons who *increasingly* reflect the life of Jesus; such people are *trustworthy* examples of genuine love to God and man. They have determined not to yield to rebellious, sinful desires, and when they do slip, they, in their regret, fall back on the gracious arms of their Lord, who offers everyone both pardon and power.

This life pattern is described in biblical terms such as "maturity," "the stature of the fullness of Christ," and" righteousness." Thus, *perfection,* as we use the term, *does not* refer to a state in which a person is beyond temptation or the possibility of sin, any more than Jesus, man's Example of perfection, was immune to temptations and self-indulgence.

Neither do we mean that the perfection set before Christians suggests a state in which no illnesses arise or no mental mistakes, such as in mathematics, are made. Because God is fair, He does not **hold people accountable for acting "out of character" when their mental abilities have been seriously damaged by old age, disease, or other disasters.**

Perfection is here used in the same context as in the following statement:

> "Moral perfection is required of all. Never should we lower the standard of righteousness in order to accommodate inherited or cultivated tendencies to wrongdoing. We need to understand that imperfection of character is sin. . . .The heavenly intelligences will work with the human agent who seeks with determined faith that perfection of character which will reach out to perfection in action."—White, *Christ's Object Lessons,* 330–332.

The urgency involved in this term rests on such passages as:

> "When the character of Christ shall be perfectly reproduced in His people, then He will come to claim them as His own." (*Ibid.*, 69).

> "The very image of God is to be reproduced in humanity. The honor of God, the honor of Christ, is involved in the perfection of the character of His people."—White, *The Desire of Ages,* 671.

In real and important theological and practical differences, perfection,

as understood in the preceding quotations, is in contrast to the concept of *perfectionism.* The latter term, emphasizing an absolute point beyond which there can be no further development, grows out of Grecian philosophy and not the Bible. Perfection in the biblical sense is simply Christlikeness—combining a relationship with God such as Jesus had, with the qualities of character that Jesus manifested. Such a relationship leads to the fulfillment of Revelation 3:21—"To him who overcomes, I will grant with Me on My throne as I also overcame and sat down with My Father on His throne" (NKJV).

Although perfection is a word not frequently so translated in English Bibles, the concept of moral perfection (that is, living a Spirit-empowered, *maturing* life with *increasing* habits of overcoming moral weaknesses (sin), an *increased* ripening of the fruits of the Spirit)—is the only goal held up to all in both the Old and New Testaments and in the writings of Ellen White. To hold that the goal is unrealistic is to doubt the divine power to sustain that which God has promised.

For biblical writers, the emphasis is on *direction*; the *pursuit* of perfection will last forever—*always growing* in knowledge and *nearing* the goal of reflecting the image of our Maker more fully. In other words, "*No Finish Line.*" The Lexus auto motto is pertinent: "The relentless pursuit of perfection." On my computer are these words: "Pursue perfection but accept excellence."

One caution: those who focus on personal perfection as the primary goal in their lives are likely to experience less of it than those who make service to God and others their overriding concern.[27]

In determining what the Bible writers and Ellen White meant by the concept of perfection (whether the actual word is used or not), it is always necessary to submit to a basic hermeneutic principle: Let the meaning be found in the context.

Appendix G: "The Final Generation"

Most every Christian believes that there will be a "last" generation—that is, a "final" generation. It seems so obvious! The issue seems to be its significance. Many believe that God is delaying the Advent, waiting for something special to develop in the "last" generation and have expressed this concept as "the harvest principle."

The harvest principle is derived from several biblical concepts concerning the Advent that otherwise remain disconnected and isolated. The essence of this principle has been reflected in Adventist thinking for more than a century from such early leaders as the Whites, Loughborough, Bordeau, Smith, Haskell, Prescott—and many more since.

Distancing from many Christians who also emphasize the return of Jesus (for example, those of the secret rapture notion) the harvest principle emphasizes the *conditionality* of the Advent—that God will wait for a ripened harvest (Mark 4:29, Revelation 14:15,16)—a prepared people who will vindicate His integrity and law—and that such a people become His faithful instruments of grace as He appeals personally through the Holy Spirit and through His people to the last generation worldwide to accept His invitation to live forever.

Adventists believe that evil will abound and worsen as the numbers and ingenuity of the human race increase, but the world will not destroy itself. Nor will the increase of evil, of itself, hasten or determine our Lord's return. On the contrary, heavenly forces "hold" the winds of terror until God's people are finally identified as those who can be stamped with God's seal of approval (Revelation 7:1-3). On Planet Earth, the great controversy will be played out. Before probation closes and evil is unrestrained, men and women will settle forever any question regarding the fairness and love of God.

Some believe that Christ's return depends upon the sovereignty of God—that Jesus will return at a particular time God has set, independent of human behavior. This Calvinist thinking, contrary to John Wesley's (for example) is overruled by the larger, more expansive understanding of the "everlasting gospel," which is best expressed in the coherent, synoptic understanding of the issues in the Great Controversy Theme.

Biblical texts such as 2 Peter 3:11, 12 and many Ellen White comments such as *Christ's Object Lessons,* page 69, teach that spiritual maturity of God's people has much to do with the timing of the Second Advent. I find no biblical or White statement that contradicts the harvest principle.

After Jesus described the kind of world conditions that would exist from His day to the end, He said, "See that you are not troubled; for all these things must come to pass, but the end is not yet. . . . All these are the beginning of sufferings "(Matthew 24: 6–8, (NKJV). In verse 14, Jesus gives us a positive sign that determines the nearness of the Advent: "And this gospel of the kingdom will be preached in all the world, as a witness to all nations, and then the end will come."

What that gospel is and how it is preached is the key to last-day events. To place undue emphasis on world conditions, always in turmoil, as the chief signs of the end of the world, would be similar to a farmer saying, "I oiled my combine; it must be time to harvest the wheat." Or, "It looks like there will be a thunderstorm, it must be time to pick my corn." There is as much relationship between a thunderstorm and picking ripe corn as between distress in the world and readiness of men and women for the Advent.

The harvest principle seems to be the best explanation to unite comments regarding 1) God's eagerness to punish men and women who have "filled up their cup of iniquity" with 2) His eagerness to "thrust in [His] sickle and reap, for the harvest of the world is ripe" (Revelation 14:15, 18). God will indeed lift His restraining hand off Satan *after* He has "sealed the servants of God in their foreheads (Revelation 7:3). God will not close this world's probation until all living at a given time have had a fair opportunity to see and hear the difference between those who truly keep His commandments and those who finally say No to His appeals—they will get their way, and God will leave them alone! Being left alone, after filling up their cup of iniquity," with Satan's evil hand unrestrained, is to suffer the "wrath of God."

In other words, the harvest principle highlights the ripening of wheat and tares—the saved and the lost. The increasing clarity of God's loyalists in witnessing to the "everlasting gospel" and to their unambiguous public witness to this gospel will hasten previously curious or hesitant people into a mind-set of either acceptance or rejection of these life principles that ultimately leaves no room for neutrality.

The harvest principle demolishes, on one hand, the thought that 1) time will continue endlessly, and, on the other, 2) that God will come, ready or not! God will not change His strategy regarding how He prepares people

to be entrusted with eternal life—even though it seems that He has the right to exhaust His patience with wicked men and women who seem to be increasingly violent and self-serving.

Ellen White was instructed to say: "The great, grand work of bringing out a people who will have Christlike characters, and who will be able to stand in the day of the Lord, is to be accomplished."—*Testimonies,* vol. 6, p 129. Some generation of Adventists, and many more throughout this planet, will take God seriously, listen to His Word very carefully, and respond with a resounding Yes to whatever God makes clear in the toughest of time.

Notes:

1. A very brief summary of my book, *God at Risk— the Cost of Freedom in the Great Controversy* (Roseville, CA: Amazing Facts, 2004), 480 pp.

2. New York: Bantam Books, 1988, p. 193. Hawking is the Lucasian Professor of Mathematics in the Department of Theoretical Physics at Cambridge University, the chair formerly held by Sir Isaac Newton.

3. Oliver Sacks, M.D. (neurologist, 1933–) was intrigued with chemistry in early childhood and wrote about his utter fascination with the periodic table, especially as clarified by Dmitr Ivanovich Mendeleev. In his article, "Mendeleev's Garden" (*The American Scholar,* Autumn 2001, 21–32, Sachs wrote: "I could scarcely sleep for excitement the night after seeing the periodic table—it seems to me an incredible achievement to have brought the whole, vast, and seemingly chaotic universe of chemistry to an all-embracing order. . . . To have perceived an *overall* organization, a super arching principle uniting and relating *all* the elements, had a quality of the miraculous, of genius. And this gave me, for the first time, a sense of the transcendent power of the human mind, and the fact that it might be equipped to discover or decipher the deepest secrets of nature, to read the mind of God." This was precisely my experience when I "discovered" the implications of the Great Controversy Theme fifty years ago.

4. *Steps to Christ,* 11; *Prophets and Kings,* 311; 5 *Testimonies,* 738; 19 *Manuscript Release,* 331.

5. "The Great Teacher came to our world to stand at the head of humanity, to thus elevate and sanctify humanity by His holy obedience to all of God's requirements, showing it is possible to obey all the commandments of God. He has demonstrated that a lifelong obedience is possible."—Manuscript 1, 1892, cited in *Ibid.,* 139. *Signs of the Times,* January 20, 1890: "The only way in which He could set and keep men right was to make Himself visible and familiar to their eyes. That men might have salvation He came directly to man and became a partaker of his nature. The Father was revealed in Christ as altogether a different being from that which Satan had represented Him to be." This paragraph needs to be read and reread often, for in these few words we have the rationale for what theologians call "justification" and "sanctification." The only way we can be justified ("*set right*") and sanctified ("*kept right*") is to keep our focus on why Jesus came to earth.

6. *The Desire of Ages,* 758.

7. Ibid., 761.

8. "When Christ left the world, He committed His work to His followers. He came to represent the character of God to the world, and we are left to represent Christ to the world."—*Signs of the Times,* April 15, 1889. "God designs that every one of us shall be perfect in Him, so that we may represent to the world the perfection of His character. He wants us to be set free from sin, that we shall not disappoint the heavenly intelligences, that we may not grieve our divine Redeemer. He does not desire us to profess Christianity and yet not avail ourselves of that grace which is able to make us perfect, that we may be found wanting in nothing, but unblamable before Him in love and holiness."—*Ibid.,* February 8, 1892. "In the exercise of his sovereign prerogative He imparted to His disciples the knowledge of the character of God, in order that they might communicate it to the world."— *Ibid.,* June 27, 1892.

9. *Review and Herald,* February 11, 1902.

10. *Ibid.,* 264.

26. "God's purpose was reaching its fulfillment. Jesus was earning the right to become the advocate of men in the Father's presence."—*The Desire of Ages,* 744.

27. I am indebted to David Larson for this emphasis.

Index

Symbols

A

B

C

G

H

M